FAITH AS A DURABLE
AND REASONABLE TOOL FOR
BELIEVERS IN THE 21ST CENTURY

FAITH AS A DURABLE AND REASONABLE TOOL FOR BELIEVERS IN THE 21ST CENTURY

JOHN WENZLAU

Troitsa Books
Huntington, New York

Editorial Production:	Susan Boriotti
Office Manager:	Annette Hellinger
Graphics:	Frank Grucci and Jennifer Lucas
Information Editor:	Tatiana Shohov
Book Production:	Donna Dennis, Patrick Davin, Cathy DeGregory, and Lynette Van Helden
Circulation:	Latoya Clay, Anna Cruz, and Lisa DiGangi

Library of Congress Cataloging-in-Publication Data
available upon request

ISBN 1-56072-385-8

CIP

Copyright © 2000 by John Wenzlau
      Troitsa Books, a division of
      Nova Science Publishers, Inc.
      227 Main Street, Suite 100
      Huntington, New York 11743
      Tele. 631-424-6682   Fax 631-424-4666
      e-mail: Novascience@earthlink.net
      e-mail: Novascil@aol.com
      Web Site: http://www.nexusworld.com/nova

Printed in the United States of America

CONTENTS

INTRODUCTION

It has often been argued that *nothing is so powerful as an idea whose time has finally come.* We have seen the manifestation of this concept in various forms and fashions throughout the course of history. In this century alone we have seen this dynamic at work in numerous ways. In the first part of this century we saw how Marxism/Leninism/Communism virtually captivated and captured almost one half of the worlds population for almost three quarters of a century only to see it collapse from the inside, virtually implode, when the people themselves were no longer enamored with promises that could not be kept.

We have also seen this same principle at work in the Church. In the millennium after the emergence of the Church we saw a stagnation, even a degradation, of our belief system which did not radically change until such time as Luther, Calvin, Zwingli and others helped transform this beached whale so that it would either move forward or die. Additionally, in this century we have seen a further refinement, or as some would say *a radicalization,* of the way we do church to the extent that the chasms between the mainline denominations and the fledgling *spirit filled* groups have created a sea of *something for everyone* in our Christian religious experience.

In many ways, our world, as we anticipate the next millennium, is as how Charles Dickens so aptly put it in his classic book *A Tale of Two Cities: "It was the best of times, it was the worst of times."* How do you feel about today, yesterday or tomorrow for that matter? Have the ambiguities and complexities of living in this modern world so completely taken over your life that you are either frustrated, angry, perplexed, confused or even depressed about life in general and Christian living specifically? If so, then this book is for you! Not only does it express some of the anger that we all feel, it also goes into the frustration and perplexities of this so called high tech existence. Yet through it all, there shines a light, that still serves as a beacon for us today and that light *really is Jesus.* Yes, there really is a God and He still moves mountains and parts waters. And out of this need to feel and know that God is still in control comes this book, which in many ways is a clarion call to go to war; but unlike past ideas which have attempted to marshal the forces of believers in groups *this call goes out to you as an individual believer* as this becomes guerrilla warfare for the time ahead.

As we grow older, we oftentimes have the tendency to look back, over our shoulders, at our lives and in our reflection we see the former times as simpler, not as complex, not as emotionally draining as compared to what we presently face and endure. We view the days of our youth as times not just to be cherished but certainly more conducive to where we want to be. I don't know if this is a function of just growing older, a function of the times, a combination of factors or just a function of life.

As I look at my world, at our world, as we anticipate the end of this century and the advent of the next millennium I sometimes shudder, not just at my personal anxiety about my spiritual walk, but also about what I sense about our corporate frustration with the current state of affairs within Christianity and the realm of believers. To that extent this book has arisen out of a lifetime of frustration and confusion in my Christian walk. Having come to know the Lord at a very young age - 8 - I had, like most believers, had my ups and downs and I have noted over the years, however, that it is not just the ups and downs that create difficulties but rather those periods of going *sideways* that oftentimes provide our greatest source of frustration.

The ambiguities of Christian living are incredible. On the one hand we have a singular faith which has an individual flavor and relationship. Yet, on the other hand, it is an institutionalized maze through which we oftentimes have difficulty maneuvering. Coupled with that is an industry, *the church,* which employs people (pastors, etc.), many of whom, like our politicians are more interested in ego gratification and job security than in meeting the needs of people. Somewhere in this confusing maze, God appears - yet he becomes as elusive in our everyday lives as does peace - be it the visible or invisible.

Additionally, we have become a nation of passive believers - me included. The media has done my thinking, both critically and creatively and the government becomes a big brother as does Big Business, while the church becomes my conscience. All of the above stolidly maintain their independence and purity (well, maybe not government) and disavow that politics (or whatever name you give it) plays a role in the day to day affairs of life. As I began searching for answers to my own issues, I quickly discovered that my choices seemed limited. Ultimately I concluded that the only choice I had was that God was in control and that Media/Government /Business/Church somehow had to be subservient to the direction of God. Then I discovered something else - There is just not enough time in the day to adequately think critically about Media/Government/ Business/Church and have a relationship with God and family while still trying to earn a living and being the kind of individual that I thought I ought to be.

As I examined my belief system and looked at what was constant in my life I concluded that the only way to have a breakthrough in my life was for ME TO JUST DO IT. You know, like the Nike commercial, JUST DO IT! I was in church one day, listening to our pastor, a wonderful sensitive spirit filled man, with an obvious tender heart for people. As I listened to him it was like the Holy Spirit covered me with a blanket, saying . . . " if you want a breakthrough, not just for now but permanently . . . if you want answers to your prayers . . . its going to come from Me . . . not from a pulpit. Not from a TV. And write it down so that you can share it" Now that was a revelation to me, not because I didn't already know what the Holy Spirit was telling me, but because I got caught up in the same trash that everybody else does. Let someone or something else do your thinking, and have the relationship for you. It was at this point that I realized that I had been doing what everybody else is doing, namely shifting responsibility for my spiritual condition away from myself and on somebody else.

I told my wife, Kathy, that I was going to work through our situation, beginning Monday morning and so on August 22, 1994 I began this rather strange odyssey. And, as I began writing, I noted that many frustrations, heartaches, issues and unanswered questions came out of my spirit; things that may have been keeping me in bondage for a long time. It was at that point that I concluded that "guerrilla" tactics were needed if a breakthrough was going to come, that I needed to take back my life. Hence this book. It is not intended to be an apologetic treatise nor a blatant attack on the church. It is not designed to replace anything in your life. It is certainly is not designed to be a formula for how you should relate to God. There is too much of that going on as it is. Hopefully this book will give you some insight and, maybe, more important, the courage to have a strong, fulfilling relationship with God because that is what the Christian walk takes, courage.

If I ask questions and make statements that oftentimes sound irrational and/or sacrilegious, they are not intended to be so but they are intended to generate an emotional reaction within you. They arise from observations, feelings and indoctrinations of the years. If they strike a chord in you, then perhaps you will understand what it is that you really need to do for your own life. What is most important, however, the only thing that really matters, is you and your relationship and walk with the Lord and your relationship with your family. There is a crisis in the world today and it is not caused by external threats; it is in the heart and minds of a people who have been seduced by the sweetness of the now, coupled with the stress of the immediate as opposed to the important. So, if you feel as if you are part of the great number of those who feel disenfranchised in this world you can take back your life! But you must begin Today.

CHAPTER ONE

LOOKING FOR ANSWERS

It is common for a person to be caught up in a situation where he or she apparently no longer has any answers. It is further evident that the ensuing questions lead to some conclusions, albeit oftentimes based on faulty or imprecise reasoning. Issues such as failed relationships, the inability to move forward in a career, financial hardships, dreams that have crashed and other related baggage has become common place in our 20th Century world. There are, of course, many reasons as to why relationships crumble, families disintegrate, why careers stall or financial difficulties arise. There are additional reasons as to why difficult situations remain difficult or appear to become hopeless.

Failures, generally speaking, are a function related to 'time' among other things. A marriage, for example, is doomed to failure if the basic underlying factors are wrong or misguided - hence, it is only a matter of time before the marriage crumbles or disintegrates. Also if infidelity comes in to play during a marriage there is no question that it is just a matter of time before the relationship becomes irrevocably doomed, especially in a world where commitment has become a word that carries very little meaning. Additionally, when viewing a stalled career path, it is evident that numerous factors can contribute to one's demise. The inability to communicate with one's superior, for example, can lead directly to oblivion in an organization. If you're too direct or too reticent it is only a matter of time before your career becomes derailed. If your boss starts viewing you negatively, it is only a matter of time before you may be out of a job. Similarly, financial difficulties that begin as small nuisances have a way of becoming omens of a foreboding and disastrous future. If not dealt with early it is only a matter of time before we are faced with financial ruin. These are only a few general examples but I think you get the idea. What then are the elements of 'time' that take us down these blind alleys or into those canyons from which we never seem to emerge? Are there cosmological influences that affect us so that we are not in control of our own destinies? As Christians, are we subject to the same influences on our lives as non believers? If so, what makes Christians different in this game from non Christians? If not, why do believers seem to go through a 'time zone' that appears to erode a satisfied life even more than that of a non believer?

A question that often arises is that of the role of the Holy Spirit. How does He function in our lives in an everyday sort of way? How does he direct traffic, so to speak? If (when) answers aren't enough then there's Jesus! That's a great line but why doesn't life change when Jesus enters our life? Why is it that the answers to everyday living become more difficult to apprehend when Jesus comes into our life? Wasn't life simpler when Jesus wasn't in our life? In recent years our preachers and ministers seem to have become part of the problem rather than part of the solution when addressing this question. Why is it that their solutions (answers) oftentimes seem to be merely superficial platitudes that generally do not render answers but rather create chaos? If some people are healed, or if some find jobs, does this mean that God likes them better? That they are more holy? More blameless? Does it mean that God has it in for you if you're out of a job for a year or more - even if you are looking for work the whole time?

If your neighbor, who is not a believer, gets a good job and you're on food stamps, does that mean that God hates you? Does Satan have a bigger say over your life than you realize? After all - can God or will God? If there is any hesitation in responding affirmatively is there a problem? Who's really in charge? God or Satan? Who really pays attention to the details of an individual's everyday living? Do either of them?

When you earnestly pray and seek God's will - Why are many (most) prayers not answered? Do you even know when God answers prayers? How is it that we are so shallow that we are cognizant of the big things that God does but have no ideas of all the little things He does to keep us together? Or does He even get involved in the little things?

When it comes down to God winning or Satan winning - especially in decision making - why does Satan's way always seem to gain a preponderance? After all, can't God override this situation? Especially if we're praying for His Will to be done . . . Earnestly seeking His Face - wanting to do His will! And we get a 'zero' response. So we make another mistake. Pretty cool, huh? And then later we feel guilty because we totally messed up. What a great life! Are we having fun yet?

How can we make a good decision and know that God is in it . . . that we make the right choice . . . that we have the right answer? How many times have you felt that God was leading you in a specific direction - to do a certain thing - you even confirmed it in Scripture - you go down the path - nothing happens (or it's all bad) - now you're devastated. What went wrong? Why? Joe Blow apparently got a blessing - Is he better . . . do I have an unconfessed sin? Does he have the key . . . the formula? What's wrong with me . . . Am I stupid? Arrogant? What's the deal here? I really needed the job but Joe just moved on up the corporate ladder. He didn't need the job.

Why do some people move on and others not? Even some Christians (believers) seem to behave worse than nonbelievers and yet they move on, they move up, they become wealthy and their public testimony becomes important. How can this happen? Do you sometimes feel that everything in your life is a dead end? Why do some opportunities arise and then at the moment of apprehending them, they just vanish, disintegrate, doing a better disappearing job than Houdini? Is everything a function of sin in my life? Am I being punished to a greater extent than someone else? Should I care? Does it matter to anybody besides me?

How do I go about answering these and other questions that bombard me every day? Then, how do I go about getting action in my life . . . moving forward? How do I keep moving forward? How do I release blessings in my life and when should I be satisfied? When is it ok to want more, to dream of more, to expect fulfillment?

These and other questions become the bulwark of the following pages. I've always been a firm believer that asking the right questions are paramount to getting the right answers. Hopefully I'm asking some of the right questions.

If there are additional questions, and I'm sure there are, then maybe you will be the one to ask them as the Lord directs you. Looking for answers has become the single most important focus for believers at the end of this millennium. It is not enough anymore, for believers to merely seek a relationship with God and then others. The seeking of a relationship for the sake of a relationship is certainly not an *in* concept. We have become a generation of individuals raised to be problem solvers. Everything has become *issue* oriented and having become thus we reduce the issues of life's meaning down to the issues and problems that we feel we need to solve. So we're always looking for answers, whether it is to questions that we have been able to postulate for ourselves or to questions that someone else has raised for us. We have generated this internal need to reduce life down to a series of questions and answers and so it is on this basis that we continue to develop our relationship to God.

It is on this basis, then, that the following chapters are developed. Out of the need arising out of the deepest part of our soul. Trying to reclaim something that we feel is an inherent need, something that we feel has been lost and if we can get the answer to that one question then perhaps we can regain that feeling of belonging. Looking for answers, then, really begs the question about our relationship to God but that is really where most of us are at so it is on that basis that we depart on this rather journey. Looking for answers!

CHAPTER TWO

WHEN ANSWERS AREN'T ENOUGH . . .

Many of us grew up singing that hymn '*When answers aren't enough, then there's Jesus.*' Do you recall those words? They sure make us feel good when we sing them. The real question is as follows: what has Jesus really promised to do if we put our cares on him? Is it all for the next life or does it apply to the here and now as well?

As believers there are several choices available to us. We can live in Christ or we can live in the world Or is it, we can live in Christ (and He in us) *and* we must live in the World? Does this schizophrenic dichotomous situation dictate a lifestyle from which we can never escape or do we just escape by hoping that Jesus returns immediately?

When it comes down to everyday living it oftentimes appears as if *having Jesus* is not enough . . . and when it comes to everyday living he plays a modest role. What is it about our lives that it is not enough to believe Jesus when He says *I am the way, the truth and the life.* (John 14:6). Is it because of the implications of John 14:16 where we are told that . . . *if we bear fruit, then the father will give us whatever we ask for in Jesus name?* Or is it because there are now conditions attached that make the promises of Jesus difficult, if not impossible to obtain. If we move further along this line of thinking, we read in Galatians 5:22 that *the fruit of the Spirit is love, joy, peace, patience, kindness, faithfulness, gentleness and self control.* This sure sounds like all the things believers want and desire. Sounds like a perfect plan to me!

However, does this mean that if we are deficient in (any of) the fruit producing areas that God will not give us what we ask for? In John 16:24, however, Jesus makes the statement that we are *to ask and we will receive, so that our joy will be complete.* Where does it state here that there is a waiting period before we receive? You know, like 45 days before you get your driving license or something? In this sense I read nowhere in Scripture that there is such a thing as a waiting period. It only says 'ask' and 'you will receive.' This concept alone accounts for most of the confusion and frustration that believers encounter when they begin their spiritual odyssey.

Now the question always arises - is God only the great "order taker" in the sky? If that's all He is, then certainly our life is somewhat incomplete and superficial? We become like robots, so to speak. On the other hand, there is an interesting corollary here. Matthew. 7:11 says *if you who are evil, know how to give good gifts to you children, how much more will your father in heaven give good gifts to those who ask him.* Mark 10:14-15 indicates that *we have to be like children to enter the Kingdom of Heaven.* The interesting note here is that the requirement for faith is to be like *that of a child.* Therefore, as a child, I do not ever refrain from asking of God the desires of my heart . . . whatever they might be and whenever they might be. We should never be bashful or feel guilty - if we're going in over our head then it is up to our Father to refuse to grant our request. He can. after all, always say no, even though Jesus does not imply that as a condition of our asking -- Whatever, we ask in His name (Jesus), He (the father) will grant! So what's the problem? Why are we afraid to ask, and when we don't get an immediate affirmation or response why do we immediately think that we made a faulty request to begin with? First of all, children make dumb requests all the time. They always want more, the best, the newest, now, etc. Do we ignore or reject our children when they make ridiculous requests? Of course not! Are we sometimes exasperated with them? Certainly! How do we generally deal with our children in situations such as these? Well, for starters, we generally love them unconditionally, don't we? And while we reprimand, chastise, teach and provide for them, we never stop loving them and we always give them a response. And that's the way scripture teaches that our relationship with God is.

My son went off to college a few years ago. At that point he decided that he wanted to give Division 1 football a shot. He wasn't very big, in fact, he was a late bloomer. He didn't start growing until he was a junior in high school and then he shot up from 5'2" to 6'2" - over night it seemed. Unfortunately, his weight trailed his vertical growth by several years. At any rate he became a walk-on at his college. He didn't start; he only worked with the practice squad. By the time he departed the program, after two years, he never did get off the practice squad. At the time he left football, my wife and I were extremely frustrated with his decision to quit the program. At least that's what we concluded he was doing - quitting! He had a lot going for him at the time. He was in a reasonably controlled environment, (NCAA rules generally require some kind of monitoring), he ate well, had good tutors available, actually spoke to numerous high school groups (as an athlete), but he rejected the lifestyle and the commitment it required. Here we thought that the potential for his advancement was great and he turned it down. We were very disappointed but did we stop loving him, even when he snubbed his nose at what we thought was a golden opportunity for him? Of course not!

God, as our father, treats us in a similar way (except perhaps more rationally). When we don't do according to what He desires for us, does He reject us? No! In Romans 8:1 we read that *there is now no condemnation for those who are in Christ Jesus*. We are, after all, no longer under the law. So no matter if we do something (or don't do something) God does not reject us either. More important, as we do with our children, He still moves with us, through the hoops that are placed along our life's road. As new dreams arise, just as we support our children in their quest to achieve them, so does our father in heaven aid us in the fulfillment of those dreams.

So, I guess to some extent, God is the 'great order taker' in the sky. In one sense it is His job to provide for His children. The problem arises when you search Scripture and the conclusions that are drawn regarding what God may (will) or may not (will not) do. In Psalms 37:14 we read that *if we delight ourselves in Him, He will grant us the desires of our heart*. On the other hand, in the New Testament we read how *the heart is deceitful*. (Romans. 1:24; 13:14, Ephesians. 4:22). Furthermore, in James 4:3 it says that *when we ask we don't receive because we ask with the wrong motives*. Sounds very confusing to me. Downright contradictory in fact! As I lay this thing out it seems to go logically as follows:

1. Old Testament. God will grant you the desires of your heart if you delight in him - sounds good to me.
2. New Testament. Your heart is evil - the only thing you could ever desire is evil, therefore God will not grant you those desires, because all you're getting involved in is self gratification.

Now I know that the human heart is deceitful. But don't we get a new heart when Jesus comes into our life? Doesn't the "counselor" whom John talks about in John 14-15 have any say in this matter? In John 15:26 Jesus says that the *Counselor will teach us all things and will remind us of what he (Jesus) said*. Doesn't that kind of put us back on course, so that at least we can ask and believe that God will grant us our requests. I do not find anywhere in Scripture that we have a learning curve to overcome before the Holy Spirit considers us ready to ask with the right motive(s). If we go too far down this trail we find ourselves aligned with the Gnostics, who were bounced out of the church because they felt that the only way we could achieve perfect union was to have some special knowledge because we as humans were too stupid, depraved or egotistical. We need to remember one thing. We're children, right? Children mess up! So how do we overcome this obstacle? It's becoming akin to a 3-ring circus or a Chinese fire drill - the Bible seems to be arguing what appears to be a circular philosophy and all we know is that our prayers aren't answered and that we are dying on the vine. What's going on here?

Pastors oftentimes argue from a superficial, simplistic platform and oftentimes without substance. The problem is that the solution really is quite simple. The issues arise with the responses given to the "no-answer-to-my-prayer" syndrome. Typically the retort is 'there's sin in your life.' There is something unconfessed here. There is a stronghold somewhere that is keeping a blockade around your prayers. Hogwash! I'm a child, remember? A child of God, to be sure, but nonetheless a child! Now, it seems to me that the only way out of this dilemma is if I am perfect. Unfortunately, most of us would agree with the Apostle Paul who says in Philippians 3:12-13 . . . *not that I have already been made perfect but I press on. Brothers, I do not consider myself yet to have taken hold of it. But forgetting what is behind and straining toward what is ahead, I press on*. The fact that I am to become perfect, as Christ is perfect, is my goal, my dream, my desire, my ultimate reward. Whoops! I guess that means my prayers aren't going to get answered - I am not perfect, therefore if something is slightly off kilter my prayer doesn't get answered. Oh, Oh! What now?

There are several dynamics going on here that need to be explored. The very reason for my writing this is because I do not believe in the false guilt that is being heaped on God's people, either through errant biblical interpretation, misapplied principles of the kingdom, wrongful ascribing of power to Satan or just to downright stupidity.

One of the great principles laid down in Scripture is that we are all Priests. With the advent of Jesus, our High Priest, we can all enter into the presence of God - and we do - praise his holy name! This principle also represents one of the great hazards of the faith. On the one hand, if we blindly, without prayer, study, and without confirmation decide on a specific course of action then we may completely miss the boat. We could be on the wrong trail - dumb and oblivious to what's going on around us. I used to work with a man who constantly joked that he was always in the wrong place at the wrong time. He was tired of 'being at the airport when his ship came in.' That's the hazard of an incomplete understanding of God's grace and mercy. At the same time, God does not conform to our image of Him and he reacts to us accordingly - or does He?

Another pitfall in which we oftentimes find ourselves is really deep, dark and slimy. We rely on others to tell us what is the right thing to believe. Especially preachers! It is difficult to argue with the concept of 'don't-knock-the-anointed one-of-God' syndrome. The problem is that it is usually the 'anointed ones' who press on this point. As Shakespeare wrote - "me thinks thou doest protest too much." In many ways we have become a nation of schizophrenics on this issue. We're afraid to knock the preacher (lest God zap us) but when we listen to more than one preacher we find that we have been given more than one "truth" about a subject or issue. And here I am, having always thought 'that truth was truth.' How can there be more than one truth? So, rather than question the basis of a 'new' revelation, or search out the facts for myself, I quietly go nuts trying to reconcile a plethora of half-baked truths that go nowhere in aiding me in my Christian walk.

Here I am, almost 2000 years after Christ returned to be with the Father, a schizoid in my own land. I am valiantly trying to get an answer to 'my' human dilemma but, instead, I am confronted with Let's make a deal. Door 1, 2 or three? Where is the consistency of the Faith? On what do rely when I am down and out? If I rely on myself or others, I may be at the bus station when my ship comes in or I may be forced to play a slippery game of Christian 'Lotto.' So where do we go from here? Up to this point we see that God wants to grant us the desires of our heart but, as scripture teaches, our heart is totally deceitful. Therefore, because we unquestionably ask with the wrong motives, we get no answer to our prayers even though Jesus said that whatever we ask in His Name - the Father will grant. Got that? Now, any moralists reading this and (silently) commenting on the oversimplification of my statement, let me remind you of the 'leaven of the Pharisees.' Additionally, whether you like it or not, the great preponderance of people are caught up in this maze of confusion. Doesn't anybody have the guts to stand up and say, enough already! It is a problem facing the children of God today - here and now. It appears that there is no visible answer to prayer for many believers, which creates all kinds of dilemmas previously discussed.

The natural explanation at this point is the all encompassing solution. Let's blame Satan! Enter this great black Kahuna who seemingly has the power to shut down the heavenly communication links. And, when he can't shut them down, he certainly knows how to obfuscate the truth. Furthermore, all by himself, he can bring the darkness into the light. Excuse me! I always thought that this was a done deal. Not only did Jesus die, but he died once and for all . . . but he arose again! So what's the problem?

The problem is that we are always looking for a scapegoat. Flip Wilson, in his famous sitcom of the 70's, when in the character of Geraldine, created an ongoing cliché when he used to say, "the devil made me do it!' To some extent that is a true statement but it is basically misleading. Satan may be the tempter in that he presents the glories of this world to us. Then again, much of what he presents is just ordinary stuff that we encounter in everyday life experiences. You need a job - presto - one becomes available. Is it Satan or is it God? Interesting question, isn't it?

When something good happens to us it is always God, never Satan, right? Strange, but Satan never puts anything good in front of us, does he? We are never tempted by the pleasures of this world or by things we cannot have. Only when we don't get what we ask for does the possibility of it being Satan ever enter into the equation. Then we're really sorry that our 'blind' ambition took over and now Satan can use this (false guilt) to really drive us into the ground and out of fellowship with God. Are we really so naive to think that God doesn't know when our own selfish desires got us in this screwed up position. Boy, did we get that screwed up! Without even realizing it we got the basic principle reversed. God's highest and best for us is to be in full fellowship and harmony with him; blessed with all the goodness that our psyche's can handle. Anything other than that is our own desire or the temptations placed before us. And the sad thing is that we hardly ever ask God if what we're thinking is from Him, from Satan or just our human weaknesses taking over.

So how do we deal with the issue of Satan at this point? The first implication, from Scripture, is that (1) *we now have the power to trample on snakes and scorpions and to overcome all the power of the enemy.* (Corinthians 10:18) and (2) *in the future we will see him thrown into the Lake of Fire.* (Revelation 20:10). So, there really is a certain NOW and then, an already but not yet dichotomy in relation to Satan.

It is true that Satan provides the temptations for man to do evil (Ephesians 4:27, 6:11). It is also true that Satan is a created, although not a human being (Ezekiel. 28:15). So how does he hold sway over us? How does he manipulate us so that we can be entrapped by his wiles? Remember, the temptation is not primarily of the outlandish or those things that are beyond our grasp. Satan, quite simply, takes the good things of God's creation and places them before us. I am convinced, as a general rule, that the human spirit knows the boundaries with which it is confronted. Some are born to dream gigantic dreams while some prefer to remain where they are planted. As a result, what we sometimes view as outlandish may in reality be commonplace. The difficulty arises when we hardly ever stop to examine whatever is put before us, whether it is right for us or not. If it looks good, feels good, tastes good, then it must be good! Ergo, from God!

Our world is an interesting place. Have you ever wondered about what your life would be like if you were rich or famous, handsome or beautiful, smart or talented? What is it about the human spirit that does not accept the here and now as 'good'? When I first began flying on a regular basis, it was a real treat for me to fly over cities such as New York, London, Los Angeles, Rome, etc. As the plane passed over these cities I would gaze at the rooftops of those thousands of homes, and, once in a while, I'd muse about what might be occurring at a particular home at that particular moment. How would my life change - or the lives of the people in that home - if I were to appear at their door right now? If nothing else, my life and that of those individuals would change forever, if for no other reason, than new elements had entered into each of our lives.

However, all we can really do is play the hand that is dealt us. Speculation about what could be different is just that, idle speculation. In many ways life is a game (pardon the card game metaphor) but it's true. The people in those homes that I mentioned just a few sentences ago likely do not even know that somebody, at one time, while flying over their home imagined who they might be or what was happening to them at a particular moment. Life just went on. They dealt with what they had. Only when confronted with something new would an adjustment be made.

Job was an interesting individual; a very wealthy individual, I might add. He went on about his business and did his thing. He worshipped God, offered up sacrifices, played with his grandchildren, whatever. Then, one day, as we read in Job 1:8ff, Satan got involved in the life of Job. Thereafter, Job's life was never the same. Things changed! All of a sudden we are confronted with major changes. How we deal with them will be discussed later but for now it is worthy to note that not everybody is subject to the calamitous events that affected Job. Most of us are subject to the insidious vagaries of everyday life which keeps us preoccupied.

Is there enough money to buy groceries today? Will there be enough money to pay the rent or mortgage on the house? How about shoes for the kids? The list goes on and on, doesn't it? Life's a struggle isn't it? Why does the grind of everyday life just keep going on? I keep praying, earnestly, but nothing seems to change. My pastor says that if I tithe then God will bless me financially! I try, but I'm still always short. Too much month for the money I have. Sound familiar?

There are an awful lot of people out there who believe that this question can be reduced, and hence answered, in a formula. Sow your seed today and it will come back 100, 60, 30 fold! God loves a cheerful giver! I don't need to go on, do I? You've heard it all before and while you've tried to tithe, all you've done is found yourself deeper in the hole. Rather than have your problems solved, you now have less month to work with. Sound familiar to you? It does to me!

In my own life a number of things have happened over the years. Some of it good, some of it not so good. If I were to follow the logic of the average pastor, I should be independently wealthy and retired by now. In 1990 after returning to the U.S. from spending some time abroad I suddenly found myself without any form of gainful employment. I was now eking out a living and prospects to move on were dim. The marketplace for a 40-year-old was very slim; even for a well educated, experienced individual such as myself. I was unemployed for a period of almost two years. I tried a number of things - including starting my own business (again). It was during this period that I learned several things about the world that I found somewhat disconcerting, but a reality nonetheless.

The first thing I noticed was that there are the haves and the have nots. It seemed very simple to me. Then I looked at the Christian scene to determine if another pattern was discernible. There wasn't. The community of believers seemed to be pretty much divided the same way - the haves and the have nots. What was the explanation for this phenomenon and does this have an effect on my life? Frankly, it wasn't until recently that I put all the pieces together but here goes - if I offend anyone, I am truly sorry. However, I have noticed one thing over time and that it is perception that counts in the world. That is reality for most people. And that should not be reality for us. Try to get past your perception and you will begin to live in a new world.

Jesus really is the answer, even when the logical explanations don't always seem to pan out. You cannot live your life in a superficial vacuum. The answer to your needs is found in one source, Jesus, and your response to him, other than merely as the answer man. It really does go deeper than that. I mentioned earlier, that the proper questions are essential to receiving the correct answer. Look at your questions, then decide if those are the real questions that you have. If they are, then God will answer them. If they are not, then it is up to you to formulate the correct question to ask so that you can obtain the desires of your heart. It still is a function of you being a new creation, and it is that new creation that lives and breathes in harmony with God and His will for our lives, including the providing of answers to the questions that really matter.

CHAPTER THREE

SHREWD AS SNAKES

If we're going to let Jesus be the answer then it is essential that we begin our journey by being proactive and discerning in our lifestyles and our walk. It is manifestly evident that Christians (believers) generally are no different from non believers, at least in an outwardly observable sense. We all have similar needs and desires, similar goals and aspirations in many cases. We all are subject to meeting the basic needs of life. Things such as food, shelter and clothing. There are, however, many successful people in our world, both Christian and non Christian. What is it that separates successful Christians from those who are still aspiring to success, even if it is success by a worldly standard?

Successful Christians, by and large, are different. Besides being good at what they do they portray a sense of being able to compartmentalize their worlds. Now, I don't want to give them any more credit than they are due but the facts speak for themselves. They have accomplished much and they should be recognized for their accomplishment. But the more pertinent question is, what is it that they do differently from the rest of us, if anything? If they are successful because they intuitively perform better on a higher plane then they are truly better than I. On the other hand, if they map out their strategies, goals and objectives, as many of them do, then they certainly understand the principles of the Kingdom better than the average Christian. In any case, let's try to analyze what it is that successful people, both Christian and non Christian, do.

The first thing I noticed is that most (financially) successful Christians really do pay attention to details. What does this mean, paying attention to details? (This phrase is bandied about so much that I'm not sure that any two people view this statement in exactly the same way.) In its broadest sense it implies that, both in concept and in reality, nothing is left to chance; it is all thought through in advance - all of the potential ramifications as well as step-by-step procedures as to how the objectives will be accomplished.

In my judgment, an individual's spiritual/personal life needs to track pretty much the same way as an individual's professional/business life. Now, there are some real issues here! Namely time! As God lays down the opportunities He does so in a time vacuum. He is not bound by space and time as we are. On the other hand, he created us in a world of space and time because we are accountable (see Matthew 25:15-30) for what we do with the allotted time we have.

Bear with me here - I don't want to lose you now! We never have the time to do what is necessary or what we dream of. We always have to make the time to accomplish anything of value. Ellen Degeneris, the comedienne, was quoted as saying that *if you're not doing what you want to be doing then you probably don't want it bad enough.* Satan cannot take things away from us (because we always get them back) but he can and does rob us of time. Let me illustrate. I love watching television. My wife will confirm that there was a time that I could have been (maybe was) a couch potato. When I get home from the office - on goes the TV - I especially like sports and action type programs. I must be a frustrated gladiator of some kind. Nonetheless, that's what I do (or did) - maybe three/four hours in the evening, every evening! In fact I've gotten downright ornery when I've had to do something constructive like take out the trash. Then, when I evaluate what is happening (or not happening) in my life, I find a big zero. My relationships with my family, my spiritual life, my job - everything. A big zero. It all takes time!

To be successful in life it is necessary to pay attention to details. The energy will flow to where you direct it. It is true that you cannot do a number of things successfully at the same time. Try thinking of God and last night's ball game at the same time. It won't work. However, you can compartmentalize different issues and then work on those issues independently. It's like having several things going on simultaneously, but on parallel tracks. You can only operate one train at a time but you *can* jump from train to train. Successful people know how to do this and they always know where they are. They are organized and know that all the events require their attention.

A successful businessperson pays tremendous attention to the details of his or her business. You don't fly by the seat of your pants if you want to be successful. Every move is thought out, and/or discussed with a trusted advisor. The issues are also brought before the Lord who can then confirm or rejects for us. A business, a job, a career is really much like a chess game - or any game of strategy. In many ways it can be viewed as a battle or war. How should I proceed? What are the ramifications of this decision? What are the elements involved? What happens if this or that occurs? Do I like that outcome? Can I accept it? Does it work for me? What about the other alternatives? Do they work? Do I like these outcomes better or are they worse? Finally, does this decision honor the Lord? With the exception of the last statement, all of the questions reflect the elements necessary to achieve success. It's paying attention to detail. Without that last statement, however, all that occurs is that we have achieved self gratification; we have not honored the Lord, just ourselves.

Jesus and Paul speak directly to this issue. In Matthew 10:16, while speaking to his disciples, Jesus tells them that *you are being sent out as sheep amongst wolves; therefore, be as shrewd as snakes but as innocent as doves.* The apostle Paul relates it on a more personal level, where he says in I Corinthians 14:20 . . . *In regard to evil be infants, but in your thinking be adults.*

Be shrewd in your workplace - in your business - in your home - in your relationships. Recognize the game that is being played. Learn the rules and then play the game. For the longest time I refused to recognize (admit) that life really is a game. In my naiveté, I always believed that the church of all places should be pure and holy. If I could somehow keep myself aloof in this environment then I would be all right. After all, God could then bestow his blessings on me because I was pure. First of all, that is self delusion in the worst way. The church is probably the worst example of 'freedom from politics' that is evident in our world. It started during Peter and Paul's time, extended through the period of the early church and is evident and manifest in the church today. Jesus even recognized this when he saw the religious people of the day and said in Matthew 13:11 . . . *that is why I speak in parables.* He (Jesus) set new rules for the game. He set in motion the wheels for a new game. That is why, in everything we do, we must recognize the game, learn the rules, play fairly and play to win.

Whoops, I guess I shouldn't have made that last statement . . . and play to win! After all, doesn't winning imply that someone loses - and in that case doesn't this somehow negate the biblical principle of 'loving one's neighbor?' It can! It usually does. But it shouldn't nor does it have to!

There are several points that need to be addressed here - the issues of graciousness, pride and arrogance! My wife always has to remind me that my arrogance has cost me - that my pride is difficult to accept (it is also difficult for the Lord to accept), that she wishes I were more gracious in my dealing with people.

In both Proverbs 8:13 and Isaiah 13:11 we see references to what God thinks about arrogance and pride. It's very difficult for a boisterous, gregarious guy like me to be subdued when the adrenalin is flowing, when I'm pumped up and I want the world to know what a great guy I am and what a great job I'm doing. You know, we men are so full of ourselves - It oftentimes takes a woman to point out that we are full of ourselves, selfish and self serving, boorish and otherwise obstreperous, We don't like what people say and think about us, we take offense but yet we never learn. Pride and arrogance leads to flattery and the apostle Paul warns us in Romans 16:17-18 to *stay away from those people who flatter.*

At any rate, back to winning - even Paul stresses in 1 Corinthians 9:24 that we should *run so as to obtain the prize.* I know that is difficult at times. We oftentimes say, how can I can win or even finish the race when I don't ever seem to be in it. That is really a cop out. By virtue of being in this world we are all in the race. It may not be the race we want but we're in it. It may not always feel like it, but then we should know that feelings can't always be trusted nor should they be. They mislead and they hinder. When you're down and out, you don't feel like you're even in the game, you don't even know what the game is. You want to compete but don't even know how difficult it is. When you're up to your eyeballs in mud and the alligators are nipping at you it is difficult to remember that your first objective was to drain the swamp.

Nonetheless, despite your current situation, your only starting point is what you have, where you're at, who you are - right now! When we're looking for answers, we want responses right now. We act like children and we are - the only time that acting in this manner is inappropriate is when we think we no longer are children. Because, it's when we start acting like adults a.k.a. 'spoiled brats' that Satan gets a stronghold over us and that our victory is then already lost. Sometimes we lose before we even get into the game we think we want to be in. In one sense then, this is what Jesus was talking about when he indicated that a person had to be like a child to enter into the Kingdom. Children, at least, are teachable whereas adults think that they know it all.

For eight months I have been working on developing a major business deal. I've been in this particular industry for a number of years and have had more than my share of success. Lately, it seems that whenever I get to a door that may portray success (finally) I get stymied - it's like hitting a brick wall! All of a sudden, nothing! Has that ever happened to you? Talk about discouraged. I've been going nuts. What's going on here? Am I going to die on the vine? For a while it got so bad that my wife looked at me one night and remarked that our lives seemed to be a reflection of corpses; that we're buried. Her comment was true. While my heart still believed that the future was bright, my mind had shut down and concluded that the only way I was going to succeed was by making a pact with the devil.

As a believer I know that we have a choice in life. I also know that God is always faithful even when, most especially when, we are faithless. (2 Timothy 2:13) This is tough to remember when everything looks bleak. In fact, at that point the discouragement is such that a pact with the devil, an arrangement to get out of this dilemma, looks like an awfully good alternative. I have, however, noticed one thing about this notion over the years. If you are a believer, washed in the blood, and living under the blanket of the resurrection then Satan doesn't want you! You see, you are of no value to him - what he wants is a defeated Christian, not a dead one! He doesn't want converts as much a he wants numb, ignorant prideful, arrogant Christians, the kind of people who can misrepresent the Gospel - as well as misapply it.

My wife always keeps telling me that there has to be more to the Christian life than just the hope of eternal life. While that is more than most people have, it is not enough for us as Christians. As believers we have every expectation that our lives should be victorious, that our dreams should come true and that value and purpose for living exists - both for the future and for the here and now! This is undoubtedly one of the great dilemmas facing people today. Meaning! In life! Eternal life ought to be enough but it isn't. We want more. And what's more, God wants more for us. Is that natural - normal - reasonable? Apparently for the early Christian church it wasn't, as history records countless numbers of people retiring to a life of monasticism and seclusion, awaiting either the arrival of our Lord or waiting to join him by ceasing to live in this world physically. But as history records, Jesus didn't return and so many people missed out on so much that God had available for them.

What is it about being productive that drives men - not all men - but certainly enough of us? If we do a word study on the word 'life' it certainly can become a depressing experience, especially if we are looking for an indication that there is more to life than just 'eternal life.' Throughout Scripture the general tendency is to relate the word 'life' in a transcendental sense. The hope is for the future and that is where the emphasis is placed. We get so many references to eternal life and metaphors relating Jesus to life that we oftentimes become afraid to look at our earthly existence in any other way. There is no meaning, except after we die. Boy, that is depressing! And then we have preachers/ pastors who dwell on the eternal so much that Satan has fertile ground on which to prey. We feel guilty if we view our lives in any fashion other than bringing the lost to the Lord. Now, don't get me wrong here, the spreading of the Gospel, the Good News, is very important and is essential to fulfilling the Word. However, in my observation of mankind I have concluded that there are a lot more Moses' around (but without his education, training and background) who don't have an Aaron as mouthpiece and more importantly do not have the direct pipeline to God that they claim. What are these guys supposed to do now? Stay in bed all day, play golf or go fishing? No question but that might be the best thing for all us of us. Nonetheless, they create all sorts of difficulties for us through faulty reasoning but wide open mouths.

My study of Scripture reflects that we are expected to be fruitful - we are to bear fruit. In fact, if we don't bear some fruit then we are subject to being cut down (Matthew 3:10). Sometimes the division of labor occurs by decree, sometimes by the assignment of certain gifts, other times by just happening to be in the right place at the right (or wrong) time. Nothing, however, occurs by chance and whatever the method of conscription we are ordained to (1) work for a living (Genesis 3:19) and we are to be fruitful in this life (Luke 6:43; Genesis 35:11) The fruit is not only (and always) spiritual fruit, even though that is important. In the Garden of Eden, man's task was very simple - take care of the Garden. (Genesis 2:15) Our task in this world is always two fold - (1) to take care of needs such as food, shelter, clothing and (2) our relationship to the Almighty. This notion becomes further refined in New Testament thought where we are to bear good fruit (both literally and figuratively). Matthew 7:17. Much of Jesus' teaching was done by way of parables and while much of the intent was to breeze by the academicians of the 1st Century University of Scribes and Pharisees, much of the intent was also to relate to the people in a manner with which they identified . . . in idioms about the land. Because Jesus used agricultural terms, his teaching was understood by the mainstream citizenry of agricultural Israel but the technical terms used went right over the head of the intelligentsia. You don't have to be a rocket scientist to understand that a garden needs to be watered, that weeds need to be pulled and that limbs need to be pruned if you want to reap the best harvest. Little wonder that the academicians had little regard for Jesus and what he taught - he didn't speak their language. He ostensibly ignored them in favor of the common man of the day. Interestingly enough, they (the academicians) could have learned the lingo had they so desired but they refused to come down to where the action was at. Sometimes I wonder if we haven't reinstituted the 20th Century University of the Scribes and the Pharisees.

Now we do not live in an agricultural society anymore. In fact we have almost moved through the industrial age and are on our way to becoming fully immersed in an information/ technological age. Nonetheless, the principle remains - take care of the Garden. We have probably changed this to TCB - taking care of business! Be proud of your work. Remember, you really do race to win, so don't do a slip shod job; be the best.

It is an oftentimes general but alluded to perception that if we do such a good job, that we will make others (notably bosses and co-workers) look bad. Now, this becomes doubly compounded if the 'others' are also believers. After all, we're not supposed to offend them are we? Nowhere is it written that we are to be slack in our drive, in our desire to do the best possible job. What we need to do, however, is ensure that attitudes such as pride and arrogance don't enter into the picture. It is these attitudes that destroy relationships and directly lead to such issues as 'loss of jobs', etc. It is very unusual (except perhaps in cases of corporate downsizing or failure of businesses) that a person loses his or her job if an attitude of graciousness coupled with hard work has supplanted arrogance and pride. If you're taking care of business that will never be a problem. Even if a business is failing, God will grant you the insight to see that failure in advance so that you can do something about it. So don't give anyone an opening to drive a wedge of destruction in your life. It is your responsibility to see that doesn't happen. I keep coming back to I Corinthians 14:20 - *when it comes to evil, be as infants but in your thinking be adults*. Sometimes I'm not sure that I like this verse because when viewed parallel to Matthew 10:16 the expressions *shrewd as serpents* and *thinking as adults* become co-related. But that is our admonition, indeed our driving force, our by line - try it - and while you, like me, may hate the notion you will soon agree that operating on this level is essential to living an effective, fulfilling and prosperous life.

Now that this concept is out in the open, how do we accomplish this. How can my job, my marriage, my family and my relationship with God and all the added dreams and desires all be developed to the extent that I can live this fruitful, joyous, fulfilled and prosperous life. While it sounds good, it also carries with it the notion of impossibility and to some extent a reaction of incredulity is justified. The shear magnitude of the thought alone is overwhelming. You can almost feel the energy drain just thinking of the issues involved trying to live such a life.

We do live in a 'me' world. In fact, the 1980's have often been described as the 'me' decade. Whatever it takes to make 'me' happy! The focus was always on the self. While I'm not sure that this fixation with 'me' was altogether that new, what was new that it was so openly practiced and adhered to. As a result we saw a number of things happen. More people got rich as it was now socially acceptable to actually pursue money. Additionally, on their way to pursuing the god of money, more people also went bankrupt. This decade also saw more people get divorced. It's natural, whenever, you start to focus on yourself you're going to satisfy yourself. Whatever it is, whatever it takes! The only question is who and what is left crushed on the road that we so rapidly traversed over to achieve our objective - me! And Christians were no exception. I was no exception. But thankfully, God answered the prayers of a faithful and loving wife who heeded the admonitions of the Lord. Even then our road to recovery was one of difficulty and filled with snares and pitfalls. But not every Christian was as lucky as I. Many fell, mortally wounded. Some good examples are the Televangelists who not only fell from Grace but fell from life. Some of the stories are almost too painful to recount and as I share with you I'm sure that you have names and faces and events that you can substitute, literally making your own story.

I have a friend whom I knew from college days. A genius really. Today he would be referred to as a geek; back then he was a nerd. (But then I know some wealthy and powerful nerds.) As my friend climbed and clawed his way to the top it became evident that he possessed something special. In fact, it was flattering to be in his presence. The accolades were heaped on him. It soon went to his head. He was a preacher and I remember a pastorate of his, fairly large, where his preaching was so anointed that there was literally 'no room in the inn' when he preached. People would come from afar to hear the message of God preached by this man. People literally blocked the aisles, even on Sunday nights and Wednesdays. What power! What anointing! Then one day it was over! He concluded that God had called him to a bigger and better place. You know, as I reflect on this situation, his preaching was still strong. Talent is not easily thrust aside. But the anointing was gone. One day he did reach the pinnacle of *his* dreams and he became pastor of one of the largest churches in America. Almost 30,000 members. He had satisfied 'me' . . . but the anointing was gone. And as we all know, *pride comes before disgrace.* (Proverbs 11:2) It wasn't long and his pride got in the way of his calling and he left the pulpit in a huff. It's only been a couple of years but the pursuit of 'me' resulted in a failed marriage, a broken home and a career that lay in tatters. Today he no longer has a ministry and is remarried. The results of the 'me' decade. The legacy left behind is truly devastating.

Me - that wonderful word, that describes who I am, what I'm about. That word that leads to utter destruction!

Have you ever heard the expression 'plan your work and work your plan?' Isaiah 32:8 says . . . *the noble man makes his noble plans.* Proverbs 19:21 says . . . *that many are the plans in a man's heart, but it is the Lord's purpose that prevails*. Proverbs 16:3 says that *if we commit to the Lord whatever we do,* *that our plans will* succeed.

So in relation to the Lord, your family, your spouse, your job, your dream it is no sin to plan it out. The prophet Joel indicates that our dreams come from the Lord. In fact the oft quoted portion from Joel 2:28ff (and later reiterated in Acts 2:17) is too important to just refer to it.

...and afterward, I will pour out my Spirit on all people. Your sons and *daughters will prophecy. Your old men will dream dreams, your young men* *will see visions. Even on my servants, both men and women I will pour out my* *spirit in those days*. While Joel was referring to the final days, the messianic age, Peter (in the book of Acts) was clearly being reflective of the church age and we see this in Acts 3, 10 & 13.

It's O.K. to have dreams and when you do, have big ones . . . for God! But don't shirk your responsibilities for your dreams. It takes time to build a relationship. Now a days many families have separate telephone lines for their teenage children because they find that these kids spend literally hours talking to their friends. What are they doing? they're building relationships! They're communicating. (Oh, oh! If you've ever listened to such a conversation you really begin to wonder what's being said, but that's not the point, is it?) How much time have you spent with your spouse - your child - your friend? It seems to me that we have overdone the bit of spending 'quality' time as opposed to 'quantity ' of time. God spent a lot of time with His friends Moses and David and nowhere does it imply that it was only quality time. After all, how long could it take for God to etch out the ten commandments on some granite? What else did they do for those 40 days and nights. It seems to me that before one gets to have quality time there is a lot of quantity of time that needs to be put into the relationship. But that's not fair, you say, after all David was a King, he had no concerns for basic survival such as I do! If you believe that you'd better reread the Psalms. And Moses, he was the leader. Leaders are supposed to do that sort of thing. I'm just a nobody, so the rule doesn't apply to me. Wrong - if you're a believer, you are first of all a 'somebody.' In Romans 8:17 we read that we are *heirs of God* and, according to Galatians 3:29 we are 'heirs of the promise.' Now, don't tell me you're a nobody. Secondly, as Jesus says in John 15:15, we are his friends, but we must also follow his commands. Oh, oh you say, that's where the catch is, I knew there had to be a catch, there always is. True. In verse 17 we see what the catch, the command is . . . 'love each other.' It takes time to love. But time in this sense isn't necessarily reflective of quantity but is indicative of quality. It costs no more to be kind than rude; it costs no more to say a kind word than a nasty one; it takes less energy to smile than to frown. While these are all aspects of quality, they do not happen by themselves because it takes time!

So now you say, that's great but my job takes times. There are things I have to do. I can't just change what I do! While that may be true, you can change your attitude. Remember the old saying, it's your attitude, not your aptitude that determines your altitude. Make a conscious effort to do your job better. Try to see your job as a part of the whole picture. If you can do that, it will have meaning and will give you pride and joy in your work. If you come up with an idea that makes more money for the company don't expect a reward. It's not your right to demand more; it's your job. You never know where your creativity will take you if you let the dreams develop. Demands and unrealistic expectations kill dreams. And dead dreams are seen on the faces of people who are alive in body only. Recognition for a job well done for a new idea is not a right, it is a by product of a tree that bears good fruit. (Matthew 7:16) *By their fruit you will recognize them.* Being outstanding is not special; it is what is commanded of us. After that the law of natural selection takes over.

Now I don't want to be talking about natural selection as that rings of the concept of evolution. However, just as it true that cream rises to the top, the brightest and best do stand out in crowds. The only time this becomes a problem is if you don' t have the patience to wait for the right time. In the world of business, as indeed life, timing is everything. There we go with that word again - time! If an idea is too early to gain acceptance it will never fly, no matter how good the idea or the person behind the idea is. Conversely, being too late for the party also presents a problem. So, as you meander through your life, be as innocent as doves in your attitude to what God has placed before you, whether it is your job, your relationships or just life in general. Let God direct your thoughts and be the provider of your energy. At the same time learn the rules of the world and the games that are played in that arena. Just because you know the rules doesn't mean that you *have* to play the game in the same manner. Just the mere fact that you spent the time to learn the rules potentially puts you in a position to avoid certain situations in particular circumstances. After all, how can you develop a thorough plan if you don't know all of the aspects of a situation. Then, when you've done your research, when you discerned all of the ramifications of a particular situation, you will be able to make much better decisions and you certainly won't be second guessing yourself.

CHAPTER FOUR

A QUESTION OF TIME

In the late 50's and 60's Del E. Webb had an idea that older, retired people would rather live out their remaining years (or at least part of them) in the sun as opposed to the cold Midwest or in the rust belt. He had no idea what to expect. At first he was thinking only of a winter haven so that escapes from the cold and snow were possible. What he didn't see was that the jet airplane and fast, interstate highways really made Arizona just hours away for anyone. The world had shrunk. If Del Webb had lived a generation earlier, his dream of a mega retirement community would have fizzled. Everything in life depends on timing. As Scripture so adequately maintains, there is a time and a season for everything under the sun. Timing - be ready for it - be sensitive to God's leadership as you bathe your job, your business venture, etc. in prayer. Don't be tempted only by the money. While financial success is important, it is the not the final word. Financial success is only a measuring stick of how people perceive you, of how well you've accomplished in your objectives. But I digress!

Timing, as I said earlier, is everything in life. If you've got it, chances are that you will be successful. While we all have experienced good fortune there are several issues that need to be addressed, namely controlling the issue of timing and how the timing issue is perceived. So how do we access this crucial issue of timing. First, you've got to know the rules and then you wait until God opens the gates.

The timing issue is both simple and complex, depending on your world view. (For the uninitiated, world view is the basic philosophical system on which you operate. Everybody operates on such a system. For example, the world view of a young gang member in the inner city may be that the only thing of value that matters are the values of his/her particular group and that force/violence is the only way in which results are achieved, whatever those goals might be. On the other hand, the world view of a homemaker may be that domestic responsibilities such as housekeeping, cooking, raising of children, etc. are the primary issues while the 'bringing home of the bacon' ought to be left to someone else. These may be oversimplified, but you get the idea). So back to world view and timing.

If you're a type A personality you believe that you make your own luck. Timing is only a function of how many contacts you have made and how hard you work is what dictates results. Ultimately, the type A personality has a tendency to force issues, generally at all times. Consequently, the individual fitting this description believes that he/she both controls the issue of timing as well as getting credit for the results. Do you know anyone like that? My success is contingent on my hard work and when I achieve it I get the credit for it! Nothing like a bushel of 'attaboys' to make to your day.

The opposite personality trait seems to feel that someone else is always in control over his/her life. A boss, a spouse, a friend, a politician, whomever. They will take care of me! I'll just keep my mouth shut, do what I'm told and everything will ultimately turn out O.K. My ____ (you plug in the noun) will finally recognize my worth/value and when the money, the promotion, the whatever happens, _____ will take care of my needs. Have you noticed that the occurrence of what you're hoping for, rarely if ever happens.

Frankly, I've tried both approaches, and maybe even constructed a few hybrids in between, with some interesting results. When I tried the type A personality approach, I really achieved some phenomenal success. I have to admit that there is some rarefied atmosphere at the top of the success ladder. Two such incidents, one for each approach, come readily to mind. Let me share them with you.

My very first job out of college was with a major corporation. I'm not ashamed to say who it was, it was Xerox Corporation. The Company made great efforts, and spent a great deal of money to train me. It didn't take very long to recognize several latent opportunities within the organization. While the bread and butter of the company, in the early years, was copiers/duplicators, there was a nascent opportunity lurking in telecopiers - facsimile in the 1990's. Today, everybody knows about fax machines. Personally, I can't get along without mine. To make a long story short, I recognized the opportunity, developed a vision, worked hard and soon reaped some very substantial rewards, financial and other. My wife and I bought our first home as a direct result of those rewards. At the time I felt that I had directly affected the timing as it was my vision that allowed me to make the contacts and then sold them on the concept of facsimile. Additionally, I took the credit and patted myself on the back - did so for years! Timing - I felt that not only was I in the right place at the right time but that I capitalized on it. Nobody was going to rob me of the experience.

There is a corollary to the above story, however, and it isn't nearly as successful. Many years later, in business for myself (after all what does an A type personality do) developing and operating senior retirement facilities in the southwest. I had the right idea, the right product, the right location and I even had Five Million Dollars worth of land (with no outstanding debt) tied up in the deal. The only thing lacking was the seed money. So I went out looking for a financial partner to help me put the final pieces of the puzzle together. I produced a detailed business plan and presented a more than glowing feasibility study. Frankly, I did everything right - by the book - but no one came forth with the needed finances. Naturally I blamed it on timing. Right idea - Right Product - Wrong Time. Nonetheless, I couldn't believe it. I just knew that if I didn't make this happen then someone else would and then I would really be upset, watching tens of millions of dollars in profit go to someone else. I literally got sick thinking about it. What was wrong? Surely, I could do something about this 'timing' issue; that was the real issue, wasn't it? I was in agony, what now? How was I going to survive this failure? I had been debating the issue with family, friends and God. My world was in shambles and why didn't God respond?

It was at this point that God took the heavy timbers to me. While I've responded to many of the issues at hand the issue of time and timing remains central to any argument. There is no reason to discuss issues of prayer, being a child of God, being able to ask, etc. if we don't somehow get a final adjudication, if we don't physically get a tangible result. So, what is the key, if there is such an animal? Well, we do know one thing if we're believers, and that is that God is in control of our lives, as well as the Universe in general. In Job 14:5 we read how man's days are determined and how God sets limits. We see further in Acts 17:26 where he has determined the times for us as well as the exact places where we should live. In fact, in the 12th chapter of Job, the writer addresses the issue very succinctly. God controls the details of life, both on the large scale, Job 12:15, *when he holds back the waters there is drought* and in individual matters, v. 17, *he leads counselors away, stripped* and Deuteronomy 32: 9-14, where we read specifically in v. 13, *that the Lord nourished him with honey from the rock and with oil from the flinty crag.* When we really get down to it, Acts 17:27 tells us the following, *that men would seek him and perhaps reach out for him and find him, even though he is not far from each of us.* Deuteronomy 11:7 tells us that *the Lord is near us whenever we pray to him.*

How long then? This becomes the question that always arises. How long do I wait for the answer? This is probably the key question that believers ask, especially when the answer isn't forthcoming soon after the prayer is offered up. Is it too much to ask that at least a response be forthcoming, whether yes or no? In life one hears the comment, "I don't care if you love me or hate me, but don't ignore me." This holds true to our relationship with God - mutually, I might add. He does not want to be ignored by us just as we don't want to be ignored by him. So, are we being ignored by God when we don't receive an answer? While it's really not that simple, it's really not as convoluted as many pastors and fellow believers make it seem. It does, however, require some explanation.

We are usually led to believe that if we do not receive an answer to our prayer(s) that one of the following conditions applies (and there may be more, be creative)

1. There is Sin in your life
2. You don't believe
3. You have doubts
4. You ask with wrong motives
5. You are double minded
6. You lack trust

At this stage we all start to go nuts. In our minds we conclude that all of the above don't apply. We eliminate number 1 because *Jesus is our righteousness* (Romans 4:24) and *the prayers of a righteous man* (James 5:16) *are powerful and effective*. So why is there no answer? We keep waiting and praying, praying and waiting. Not only do we not get the answer we still get no answer. Now we're really going bananas. At this point we're frustrated, totally bummed out and don't know where to go next. Furthermore we have concluded that either God doesn't care or that we've messed up in a way that we don't even know (i.e., 2 through 6 above). Pretty nifty situation, isn't it? Only by now we're completely incoherent in thought and deed and we become supple pawns of Satan. By now we really are participating in any one of the steps listed above and things do start unraveling very fast. Not long after this we're not even asking God for anything any more. We can't stand any further disappointment. At the same time we don't want to do anything else because by now we even don't want to lose our ultimate salvation. But, one out of two, isn't bad, is it? We got our eternal life - it's just our earthly existence that's a bummer. If you have worked through all of the issues and are convinced that you are on the right track then you should *not* give up on your dream. You can achieve the objectives that you and God have mutually agreed upon. So before you slash your wrists, however, read just a little further. Help is on the way. The next section can change your life.

CHAPTER FIVE

FOCUS AND THE POWER OF SUBSTITUTION

We are all familiar with the Matthew 7:7 passage *seek and you shall find, knock and the door shall be opened.* However, it is the Parable of the Persistent Widow, Luke 18:1-5 that holds some additional insight. As we read this parable, the significant concept that arises is that 'if you stay with something long enough, then you will likely get it, even if all you've done is worn down the resistance of the individual at the other end.' Conceptually, I see this a little more defined. When you focus on something to the extent that the widow lady did you essentially do several things, all of which are important if you want to achieve your goals, to have your prayers answered. The first thing that this lady did was to determine what the real problem was - in this case the problem was an adversary. The second thing she did was determine who could grant relief. It had become obvious that she could not solve the problem on her own. After she determined what the real issue was and who could solve it for her she stayed after it until she received the relief she required.

Think about this little lady for a minute. Look at your life and at the situations that have occurred. Sometimes you received things pretty easily didn't you? Other times, you never got what you asked for and you gave up pretty easily. You kind of moved onto other issues and requests. (Kind of makes you wonder how important those issues were at the time, doesn't it?) Then there were those times that you just had to have that ice cream cone, or that particular toy. At that time there was nothing about the word 'no' that you understood. "No" was just not going to cut it. As you reflect back on these personal observations you will see many such occurrences and you will also note that you got your fair share of ice cream and toys.

If you say to yourself that you could never be that persistent, that persistence is annoying, that other people dislike that approach then I have a question for you. How do you get along in life? Are there no situations when you finally have had enough? That this is where I take my stand. You know it doesn't matter if the stand you take is to someone above you, or below you. It is the principle that counts.

When you reach the point that you're faced with taking a stand, then everything else becomes secondary. You no longer are swayed by inconsequential peripheral issues. All of a sudden a solution to the main issue is of paramount importance. You don't care about television, you don't care about talking to friends, you don't care about the fact that Sally wore a dress like yours to church on Sunday. None of those issues matter anymore. You need a breakthrough - an answer to your problem. That's all! You are now focused. And by George, you're not going to stop until you solve your problem. You now have substituted the perceived goal for the perceived (or real) problem. You are now working on the solution side of the equation rather than the problem side.

Have you noticed, that the problem side is always filled with negatives? Why? How could this happen to me? How will I survive? Why doesn't God answer? He knows my need. Etc. Woe is me! On the other hand, when you focus on solutions, your mind is focusing on possibilities, and it is the possibilities which give rise to solutions. The power of substitution is immense and it is an important lesson that needs to be learned as this concept directly affects issues relating to time. While some people do this intuitively, most generally have to deliberately set their minds to do so and this is always the better way as it allows God to do something definitive in your life. Just happening on a solution is generally not the best course for us and while we occasionally do stumble onto solutions, happenstance certainly is not a comforting course on which we ought to rely. Additionally, relying on chance really does dilute the focus and can rob us of what God ultimately may have in mind for us.

When I was younger, it seemed that everything I touched turned to gold. I could do no wrong it seemed. The biggest issues were usually related to how successful a deal was going to be as opposed to the notion or question as to whether or not it would be successful. It was shortly after the gravy train came to a grinding halt that I began to learn some valuable lessons. One of the first lessons was that God does not like to be a silent partner. Certainly God does allow one to go on without Him; sometimes it appears as if He goes along for the ride but I have become convinced that He does this only to protect us from ourselves rather than as a sign of tacit approval. Bottom line is this - God wants to be proactive in our lives just as He expects us to be proactive. The second lesson I learned was that God will not interfere with your decision making process unless you ask Him for advice. But there is an important element in this equation that needs to be spelled out so don't move on too fast. The important element of this concept is that just because you give lip service to consulting with God does not mean that you're automatically and/or immediately going to receive a significant direct response. You get back proportionately to what you put into the equation. If the decision warrants three hours of analysis and two minutes of prayer then you will receive an answer proportionate to the prayer you put into the issue. The bottom line is that if the issue is so important to you that you spend hours working through it then it stands to reason that it may take more than hours in the prayer closet to finish it off properly.

Now, does this mean that every decision needs to take three hours on your knees? Of course not! What it does mean, however, is that all decisions need to be viewed in the same light as that of the widow in Matthew 18:1-5. If the process warrants deciding on a what, a who and a when, then it likely warrants getting God involved, like now. What better person to get involved in solving your issues than God? In Matthew 10:16 we read how Jesus sends out his disciples to *be as shrewd as snakes and as innocent as doves.* As disciples ourselves, we should be admonished and exhorted by this. If Jesus recognizes what we face in the world, isn't it appropriate for us to at least look to him for guidance and direction with more than just a nod?

At the present time I am looking into buying a business. For a long time I wanted to buy into a specific business but I was somewhat reluctant to proceed. Finally, I determined in my spirit that the time was right to at least explore the opportunity that had been on my mind. As I visited with my family about the opportunity the Matthew 10:16 passage once again came to light and the Lord has used this in my life in a powerful way. In former times I might have looked at the numbers and done some statistical number crunching (after all, what does an MBA do with numbers?) Then I would have had a couple of meetings with the other principals involved and probably concluded that I should move forward if everything came out O.K. In this case, however, I was guided by the principle that I needed to think like the opposition. It is then, and only then, that I can get the real picture as to what is going on. You know, for the longest time I felt that I could go through life, be my own person, deal with other people in a judicious manner all the while under the assumption that if I was the good guy that I'll come out on top. Boy, did I get a wrong number! Not the part about ethics and judiciousness, but the implication that I'd get treated fairly. Then, I felt that if I just dealt with Christians that I would at least get a fair and honest shake. Not! In this instance, my final conclusion was that I would probably get a better shot at concluding a successful, mutually beneficial business deal with non Christians. Period! My attitude became that if I knew you were a crook, or a tough businessman, or whatever, that I could do business with you because at least I knew with whom I was doing business. Oftentimes I never did know who I was doing business within the Christian community. Talk about being all over the place in my thinking.

My reasoning developed to the point that it was like making a pact with the devil himself. At least you think you know what you're up against and we always feel better when we think we know the adversary. At any rate, the bottom line is this; be careful, be aware and diligent in all your dealings, regardless of the representations made to you. *Shrewdness like a snake* is certainly not a gift that we all desire but it is certainly one that we all need, especially in today's world. In my judgment the *innocence of a dove* corollary comes with the prudence exercised through shrewdness and through the leading of the Holy Spirit.

I keep coming back to the issue of time. How long do I have to wait before the answer - the solution - the blessing - is in hand? That is truly a good question and I'm sure that if I had an answer that could be formalized (as so many TV preachers intimate) then I would be the most popular, not to mention, the richest guy in town. The answer is not always neat, is not always direct and is always subject to the vagaries of life as well as the impatience and inconsistencies of the Faith that we bring to our lives each and every day.

Some people seem to receive answers to their prayers almost immediately while others almost never seem to get their prayers answered. Yet on the surface, both come across as being totally tuned in and committed believers. Why is that? If you talk with these individuals you would come away with the feeling that while both professed to be believers that one likely either doesn't have enough faith or has some unconfessed sin in his/her life. The last notion is the one that really gets to me. Who points the finger here? While it is likely Satan doing some behind the scenes negotiations he sure has willing participants in us human beings who love to immediately point to the s(in) word. I think Jesus summed it up best in John 8:7 where he said *if any among you is without sin, let him be the first to throw a stone at her.* While I am the first to believe that the Holy Spirit convicts of sin, I am also convinced that if we are faithful in our daily walk, that the false guilt issues reflected above become non issues. Also, if there is something unconfessed in our lives it is up to us to find out (based on the prompting of the Holy Spirit) what it is and then do something about it.

Now, I don't want to be blasé about the issue of Sin and sins, but my observations of human nature over the years, indicate that people (I'm speaking of adults here) generally have a reasonable grasp of right and wrong. And if they do something that violates the basic moral laws of God (i.e., 10 Commandments) or the laws of the land they generally have a good notion of what they're doing. (or not doing.) Without debating the fine distinctions that people often make in this area I do know only one thing and that is this - regardless of whether your sin is one of commission (I knew what I was doing) or omission (one that slipped by due to non recognition or understanding of the situation) you still have an advocate in Jesus . . . at all times. If the Holy Spirit brings something to mind where you messed up, go for it and confess it confidently knowing that it has not affected your relationship with God. Remember, the blood covered it all up for all time . . . a one time deal! On the other hand, the resurrection makes it possible to have the ongoing confidence that this one time bloodshedding of Jesus is really that.

This does bring me to an issue that sometimes is, or could be rather complicated. Cause and effect! Just because Jesus paid the price to restore us to fellowship with God does not mean that God arbitrarily suspended the Laws of His Universe. That issue needs to be addressed if we are to make any sense out of the prayer issue. First of all, God can do anything He wants to do. He can, and still does perform miracles. If He so chooses He can still part the waters and he does, He can still move stones and he does, every day, He can still make the blind to see and make the lame to walk and he does. And what we see most often is that God gives His people a new heart - a heart of flesh as opposed to a heart of stone. (Ezekiel 36:26) At the same time, while God can and does perform miracles, every day, there are still those situations that He lets continue for whatever reason. Sometimes the jams that we get ourselves into are ours to live with. If we smoke, for example, while we will not lose our salvation, we may certainly be subject to the health issues that smoking can bring on. Promiscuous sexual activity also can cause long term health problems. Drug and alcohol abuse also fit into this category as does gluttony. An unchecked temper can lead to disastrous consequences as can an unbridled tongue. You may, in fact, think of many more such issues yourself. God can, indeed, remove all of those issues from your life. But here's the catch! He may not remove the consequences of those issues as you previously misused or abused them. *He can, but he may not!* He may, for example, remove the desire for smoking, but not the lung cancer. He may temper your spirit but may not heal the broken relationship that occurred when you physically or verbally abused your spouse or loved one. *He can, but he may not.*

Lawyers oftentimes makes a distinction between problems and issues and that is something that you may have noticed I used quite often. An issue is something that appears as if it can be worked through to an ultimately satisfactory conclusion. Working through multifaceted tasks requiring the exploration of varying options requiring some choices to be made is a good example of an issue. Practically, this could involve your job, looking for a new position, etc. It could involve where to go to school or whatever. A problem, as we so often use the word, is more difficult and the image this word suggests is one that implies a limited solution at best. It usually refers to the addressing of a item of some difficulty whose outcome has already been determined and now we want to change it because we don't like the outcome.

In problems we want to change the scenarios because we don't like what we see at the end. In dealing with issues we lay out the essence of what is being addressed and then work things through to a logical and, hopefully beneficial conclusion. So be careful in your use of terminology as what you're working through may not be as difficult as you initially think. Additionally, determine in your mind if what's facing you seems insurmountable because you've already determined the outcome and don't like it or if it really is a major obstacle that looks like Mount Everest.

In the Christian sense I see burden and issue pretty much in the same way. A burden, in my mind, is something akin to a problem. There are limited choices and only something extraordinary will solve it. This could be related to something lingering, and/or ongoing consequences that we discussed earlier. There may be a solution but it sure isn't evident. In fact, only a supernatural act of grace will solve it. I would make the argument that it is these kinds of problems that Jesus talks about in Matthew 11:30; the obstacles over which we have limited or no control. Those things that indeed bind us because of what has occurred in our past. He still loves us, cares for us and forgives us. He has still redeemed us and delivered us from the bondage that created the problem but instead of removing the consequences he only says that he will help us carry it. This baggage has now become the burdens which we cannot always remove and they plague some of us until the day we die and join him in glory. Does this mean that we cannot cry in frustration when find ourselves in this position? Of course not. Does it mean that God is the bad guy if He doesn't respond in the manner that we want? No. But the flesh and Satan would sure make us believe that.

I would suggest that the focus be taken off these problems. It doesn't mean that you forget about them or refuse to pray about them. After all, they are important to you so you shouldn't suppress them. However, if you can, lighten up and find some issues that can be worked through. Where there are solutions, if even a stretch, and based on your limited human understanding, get a vision to accomplish something positive, even though the underlying problem still persists. It's the toughest thing in the world to do . . . I know. When you're up to your eyeballs in alligators, it's difficult to remember that your first objective was to drain the swamp. On the other hand, I am convinced that God's grace and mercy are explicit enough that we don't have to be fatalistic in our approach to life. Poets and philosophers often muse on the paths that their lives have taken because of choices that they have made. I am firmly convinced that God can, and does, right those choices and that He does bring us back to where we ought to be, but sometimes it is with baggage that we don't want to be carrying. All it really means is that God's plan for your life will now be fulfilled (if you so want) but with you (and with his help, if you want it) carrying that baggage. Let the baggage be a positive instrument for His glory and not a debilitating factor that tunes you out of His grace and plan for your life.

Issues are relative; it's the burdens that are tough. When we focus on issues, we can usually achieve the objective. Unfortunately, we spend too much time trying to shed our burdens rather than trying to work through important issues that need to be dealt with. Take the following example of a couple struggling through major trials and tribulations. Bad decisions in the past have created a situation where they virtually lost everything that was of importance to them. Tangible as well as intangible. At one time they had everything going for them. They did as they pleased, bought what they wanted, traveled at will, etc. All the time believing that they were doing the right thing. They went to church regularly, were faithful in their giving and generally gave evidence that they loved the Lord. Yet their world collapsed. Imprudent wasting of resources led to a total collapse of their world. It's difficult for people who have been successful to deal with issues of total collapse. They forget that there were bad decisions that may have led to this debacle but they cannot understand what happened and why. While they recognize that errors were made along the way this recognition usually doesn't occur until much later down the road. By then they are no longer issues to be worked through, but rather burdens that have seemingly gained the weight of an elephant and become too difficult to carry. So what does a person do under these circumstances besides wallowing in self pity and defeat. Tommy Barnett, pastor of Phoenix 1st Assembly of God church oftentimes admonished and exhorted his flock by saying that it is not a sin to get down, but it is a sin to stay down. But as we all know, getting up is sometimes a difficult chore, especially when we pray and don't see any answers forthcoming, whether tangible results or just a lifting of the spirits.

There are several alternatives available at this point. Satan, for sure, likes to see people get down and stay down. He likes nothing better than a defeated believer. At that point he can move onto the next person. On the other hand, you can be proactive in the process. Being proactive is an interesting concept in itself and implies some serious attitude adjustment for many Christians. Many individuals oftentimes go to the Psalms for encouragement and hope; after all, David encountered his share of adversity throughout his life. If it wasn't his own doing then it seemed as if it were others, both friend and foe, who were after him. I don't know what it is about people who seemingly have a oversupply of negative things happen to them. They always seem to be pleading to God for something. Sometimes it seems as if these individuals have more than their share of turmoil. Having a choice, I for one would rather not share in their turbulence and upheaval. Over the years I have become a firm believer in a contrarian philosophy. Frankly, I got tired of following the crowd. I noted that too many believers got down, stayed down and couldn't get back up again. Additionally, advice from too many incompetent, buffoon type Christian leaders was nothing more than superficial platitudes and hyperbole, bearing no results and creating additional negativity and destructive behavior thereby doing more injustice to our Lord.

Proactiveness implies that you take charge of your situation. You take the lead in working through the issues and problems. Dealing with significant areas of concern, especially for Christians is more than a superficial, cursory and passing SOS to God and then moving on using our own resources. It really means opening, and keeping open the channels of communication; after all our relationship with God is exactly that, a relationship. I liken proactiveness in this sense to a telephone. As Christians we are all endowed with our own personal cellular phone to God via the Holy Spirit. If the phone is shut off you can't call out nor can God reach you. Additionally, if you're on the line working on your issues by yourself then God still can't get through as He keeps getting a busy signal. If you're so preoccupied with your problems that you don't hear the phone ring God still can't get through. The object is to use the phone. First, keep it available for God to reach you. When the phone rings answer it, regardless of whether you're waiting for a return call from God or just being available for God to call you. That's the beauty of the phone, it's available for two way communications.

Prayer is an effective way to establish the initial call to God. It opens the line of the communication. There are, however, several principles associated with unceasing prayers that you should be aware of and need to apply to your life. The next few principles are crucial for effective communication but don't let the order of the principles listed be determinant in how you move forward. God may want you to start at a different point and work from there.

The first principle is found in Matthew 11:12 where we read that *the Kingdom of Heaven has been forcefully advancing and forceful men lay hold of it.* While Jesus goes to great lengths in the Sermon on the Mount to stress warm human qualities such as meekness, mercifulness, peacemaking, etc. there is the side that requires a more aggressive approach. Some things are accomplished by being passive, subdued and laid back. Other times, however, an overt, offensive program needs to be implemented. Passivity sometimes goes only so far. In Matthew 10:16 we read how we need to *be as shrewd as serpents but as innocent as doves.* Bottom line is this; if we're in the world, we need to know how to deal with the world. Nowhere does Jesus say to roll over and play dead when operating in this theater. If we are seeking the Kingdom, we must recognize that part of the Kingdom is later but that part of the Kingdom is here already. Go for it! You will find that it is not quite that simple but your life will become immeasurably more gratifying. Be aggressive in seeking out and pursuing the dreams and be aggressive in seeking out and attacking the challenges. When you do that several things will happen.

1. You won't feel guilty
2. You won't have to be envious over people that have; while you may not have (right away) you're at least in the hunt.
3. Remember you can't get if you don't ask and if you don't knock.

Don't be guilty for having dreams and desires. Go for it! Remember, mistakes will be made along the way, even honest ones. Those mistakes, however, do not negate the validity of your relationship with God. As you earnestly pray and seek God's blessing you will know if your prayers are out of selfish desires. If you believe the dream is of God, if you're convinced of his leadership, his confirmation, don't just ask for the blessing, You 'will' it to be done! Ask what role you are to play in the process and what you are to do. If nothing, do nothing. If you are required to participate then be obedient and do what is required. That brings me to the next topic, participation prayer, which I think is so important that I'm dedicating an entire section to it.

CHAPTER SIX

PARTICIPATION PRAYER

Focus and the power of substitution, as talked about in the previous section, are exceedingly important. It is the energy used in this area that moves us to levels beyond our normal levels of experience. And, while focusing on the positive is a message that everyone needs to hear it is not always enough. If we only look at the positive, we oftentimes still miss what God has in store for us. Several years ago I heard a sermon that challenged my thinking to such an extent that it dramatically changed my thinking and hence my life. Up to that point my prayer life was pretty much passive, albeit direct, consistent and ongoing. Sometimes I got results and sometimes I didn't. After analyzing and meditating on what this what this particular preacher said God revealed to me the principles that I now share with you. The result was that I adopted *participation prayer* as a part of my devotional life. The most difficult thing to learn about this principle was that participation was not always required and I had to be sensitive to when God wanted me as an active participant. All too often we receive principles from the pulpit or the TV that allegedly are all inclusive but which in reality do not apply in all situations. This is one of those times.

I love the story in II Kings 3. It's simple, yet direct. I'll not recount the story because I want you to read it for yourself. It's that important. There are three aspects to this story, however, that are important for us to remember. The first thing we notice is that when things go wrong for us, even as believers, when we mess up because we didn't work out all of the details with God beforehand, that we have a tendency to lay the blame on God. *It's always why me, God?* We never accept responsibility willingly; we always try to shift blame at any and all times. The second thing that we note in this story is that the King Jehosophat quite quickly realized the error of his ways and decided to do something about it. He recognized that he went forward without God so he then accepted the responsibility for his *sin of omission* and decided to go the source. Now it takes a big man to publicly admit making an error. It becomes doubly difficult when you're a King and you're in this thing with several other Kings. Nonetheless, Jeshosophat did just that because he recognized very quickly that he was in error. Nonetheless, he still went through the normal process of initially laying blame elsewhere rather than on himself where it belonged. The final aspect of this story rests on the conclusion and this is where we are today. In verse 17, the prophet Elisha commands the King to dig a ditch so that water can fill it. Sounds a bit like Noah and his ark, doesn't it? It also sounds nuts. Here we are in big trouble, trouble that we got ourselves into, needing God to bail us out and he wants us to dig a ditch. This, coming from a God, who could zap the enemy at any time and take care of the problem just like that. But, you know, as you read the story the underlying principle becomes clear and evident. Sometimes, God wants you to take an active part in the blessing that He wants to give you. Sometimes, getting out of the jam you got yourself into needs to be a learning experience so that you don't get yourself into a similar situation in the future. In times like these, this point can easily be missed and usually is because we feel that God should do everything, After all, like the song goes, we are weak and He is strong, right? Being a participant with God in his dealing with your issues may be the only thing that makes His power all the more real, all the more glorious and certainly a milestone in your religious pilgrimage.

In 1986 I moved my family from Texas to Arizona. The offer to make the move was irresistible. Even though I had prayed about the move I see clearly now (hindsight is always perfect) that it was me doing the moving, not God. I was tempted by the seductiveness of the offer from my partners. I'm sure you can imagine the prayer that I had offered up. It was more of a confirmation of letting God know that I appreciated his concern, that it was everything I wanted and that I certainly would be glad to take advantage of His (God's) provision. Now, I was off to take hold of this wonderful blessing. What a

God! It wasn't long after the move that the wheels came off. Before I knew what hit me my income was reduced by over 75% and I couldn't begin to meet my obligations. It was really a difficult time. Everything had come unglued. Like Jeshosophat, I began to complain, *why, God?* My wife and I began to continually and continuously pray about the situation (as well as agonized over it). Then, after a number of months of fruitless prayer, and continuous whining, I got truly desperate. I began to make more time to meet God as opposed to just fitting him into my schedule. I realized in my heart that I really was wrong. That my walk with him was so superficial, that even though I was a firm believer, that all I ever gave Him was lip service. So I continued to seek his guidance, but more importantly I began to develop a deeper relationship with him. While nothing much happened during this period, he sustained our family and kept the wolves from the door. The final conclusion of the story, however, was quite simple, very dramatic and certainly not what I wanted nor expected. Like Jehosophat and his King friends I was expecting God to dramatically reveal his power. This was not to be. Here I was, after months in agony, praying for deliverance, praying for a major miracle in life. And finally, God spoke to me. Clear as a bell. It was like a telegram from heaven. God told me, after hours of prayer on my knees, to leave my present position, such as it was, and trust Him for a new opportunity that would meet our needs. Now leaving was going to be tough as I always labored under the philosophy that something was better than nothing. I had some real difficulty responding to leaving everything, no matter how little, behind. This concept is generally true except when it is obvious that the present circumstances doom you to a perceived slow death rather than a quick one. When you finally conclude that death, either literal or figurative, is a reality under the present circumstances you might be surprised how efficiently you and God can work together. It is so difficult to let go and literally let God. Like the Kings in our story, I thought that this whole situation was nuts. Leave what I've got, it's not much but it is all I've got. Couldn't God provide first. Wouldn't that *really* demonstrate his power? That seemed much more sane to me. At any rate, after much soul searching and discussion with my wife, I did quit, and I gave my notice to leave. Just to be safe, I gave God 30 days to do his thing. I figured that even God could do something if given enough time. Here, I was literally going down for the count and I was still hedging my bets. At the time of my departure from my position, June 30, 1988 I still had no job, not even an interview and boy did I think I had dialed a wrong number. Not only did I not have a new job I was out of any kind of work. I really thought that I had lost it, that I had not heard God, but who knows, what other kind of voices. At that point the deceiver himself had some real fertile ground to work with but I did not quit believing as I was convinced that I had heard God correctly. Interestingly enough, even though I was literally in a panic mode, However, I maintained my faith in that I really did hear God. That really is the key to the entire exercise. Within 10 days I was back at work, in a new position, paying me four times more than what I had left behind. Exactly what I needed.

I had dug the ditch so that God could fill it. I had some difficulty in accepting that I had a role to play in God's plan and I certainly didn't understand it. Nonetheless I went along with the plan. Reluctantly at first, then with confidence. God performed a miracle in my life. No question about it. The miracle occurred in two ways. First God changed my heart and then he changed my world. Certainly people played a great role in the process as God does use people for his purpose. Unless someone picks up your application, or sees something about you that nobody else does, or picks up the phone to set up an interview with you it all means nothing. And you know, the Holy Spirit gives that kind of direction to people every day. People may be thinking or talking about you right now! The big question is . . . Is this the kind of situation in which God wants you to participate? Is there a ditch you need to dig? Not every situation requires participation on your part but until you determine this, with the guidance of the Holy Spirit, whether something should or shouldn't be done on your part, then you'd better be about the business of finding out. *But nothing happens until your heart has been changed first.*

This was a strange, though an exhilarating experience for me. I look back on those days with continuous praise to God. Since that time I have encountered additional challenges and I have often asked God if there was something I should do in concert with him. In fact, I kept pressing the point, thinking that this is the only way that God always operates. That is not the case, however. God is not one to be put in a box, only to be brought out whenever needed, either through the use of incantations or through a set series of formulas. Just as life is oftentimes the same yet different, so is your relationship to God. The only way to recognize how to proceed is to do so in partnership with him, getting to know him, so that your response to him is the correct one, not the one that you force on the situation. We are, after all, not robots, nor are we governed by a series of rules and regulations, nor is there a list which we can consult to tell us what to do and when. Just like a relationship with your spouse, it's a growing relationship that is never static but always dynamic, always the same yet always different and changing, as you grow.

Prayer can be a strange phenomenon. Sometimes God answers before you even ask whereas other times we feel that He never answers. Most times, however, prayer falls somewhere in the middle. The only determining factor ought to be like that of King Jehosophat in II Kings 3 - when in difficult situations, usually brought on by our own failure to initially be confident of God's leadership, it is not inconceivable that God wants you to participate in bringing about the answer. I know that the most difficult thing to do is to ask God first. Sometimes we do things that appear to be in the natural order of things only to find ourselves in a pile of trouble. That's what happened to Jehosophat, that's what happened to me and likely what's happened to you. Is there a ditch you need to dig? What is your part in the process?

Remember, it's a jungle out there and Satan does everything to drive you to self dependency, knowing that a Christian who sees himself as independent and self sufficient is not in tune with God and hence becomes a pliable tool. Additionally, however, keep in mind that not everything can be attributed to Satan; much of what happens in life is simply your human nature taking over. Regardless, of whether it is the temptation of Satan or just you driving the car, that your ultimate recourse is keep the phone lines open between you and God. Don't take the phone off the hook and at least answer when it rings. You never know when God has a suggestion for you that may well change your life forever. Communication is always a two-way street. Sometimes God calls you just like you call him.

CHAPTER SEVEN

IT'S A JUNGLE OUT THERE

Can we affect the timing of our prayers and when they will be answered? Can we hasten receiving an answer? How do we apprehend it? This is probably the most difficult question to answer because the Bible does not specifically or directly provide a formula type answer to the question. Nowhere does it say that if you do this or thus that your answer will come quicker, more definitively or more direct. As a result we are left with several choices. We can mumble through our prayers and agonize daily through our frustration, we can do nothing and hope for the best or we can develop a stronger and more personal relationship with God.

The first two options are the easy way out (though oftentimes without consistent results) while the latter requires patience, perseverance and dedication. As humans, believers, we have a tendency to go to the extremes - we either approach our prayer life somewhat flippantly or we avoid personal responsibility by developing a defeatist attitude by saying it's in God's hands, so be it. All I can say is Hogwash! (If you haven't noticed, I like that word) You can do whatever you set your mind to. If you want something, you generally go for it. Driven people do not stop until they achieve their goals (or unless they are diverted to a better option along the way). A great athlete commits himself to training so that he can be his best when the game begins.

I think of Jerry Rice, the great receiver for the San Francisco 49'rs. After 10 years in the National Football League he became the all time leader for touchdowns scored. I saw his record breaking performance on TV He was awesome. What was more awesome was the subsequent interview where in a very gracious way he accepted the accolades that came his way but yet reiterated for all the world to hear that his accomplishment did not happen by accident. He had trained for this moment his entire life. His passion had extended to year round training so that he could ready to achieve this pinnacle of success.

The principle for Christians is no different. Got a goal? Have a problem? An Issue? Take it to God! But be prepared to devote time and energy to obtaining the answer. But I don't have the time, you say. Hogwash! (There's that word again) I have a job, a family, responsibilities that need to be taken care of. So, are you the only person in the world affected by those kind of demands on your time? When I get home, like you and millions of other people, we're tired, we're whipped, we're exhausted. None of us have enough energy to do anything else, including praying. If you can't get with it in the evening then get up early before work, even if you're not an morning person. You might be surprised how much energy God grants you when you make that kind of commitment to get closer to him. While most men would agree with the concept that it is the responsibility of the husband to provide spiritual leadership in the home, they then promptly relinquish that responsibility in the name of secular and other demands and responsibilities on their time. My wife, the sage that she is, continuously reminds me that it is my responsibility to intercede for my family and our needs, that no matter what the demands on my time, that there is nothing more important than praying for my family and God's leadership in every aspect of our lives. Not surprisingly, developing a relationship with God requires discipline, whether it is to get up early or to stay up late, depending on how your personal clock works best. Remember, if you want something bad enough, you'll do whatever it takes to achieve it. This principle applies to the spiritual realm as well as every other area of your life. Scripture is clear when it says that if *we take one step towards God that he'll come running towards us*. The discipline required to have a prayer life, to get answers, to receive blessings is tough but it is infinitely rewarding.

It's only a question of time and time, as part of the human condition, is a function of cause and effect. If you want to affect the time it takes to get an answer to your prayers it is directly related to the energy that you put in to get the answer. When we look at the scripture *Seek first the Kingdom of God and then these things shall be added unto you.* (Matthew 6:33) it becomes evident that the prerequisite is for us to take the first step. The difficulty is that we take the step and then stop, expecting God to come forward, which He does. But then we do nothing else and when we don't get the answer/response we want, in the time frames that we want, we get antsy and frustrated; like kids. Doesn't it stand to reason, that if you want to keep the deal moving forward that you get and stay ultimately involved? You would do no different in a business deal. You see that through to the end if you want to achieve the desired result.

In business, as well as other areas of life, I often hear the comment that you don't know for sure that a deal is closed until the check clears the bank! Why is that? Generally, it's because we have learned through experience, throughout the lifetime of any situation, that difficulties arise that continuously threaten the resolution of the issue/problem or the finalization of the deal. If we want to achieve the desired outcome we get more and more directly and intensely involved as we get closer to the answer/resolution because more and more negatives attack the situation; many times unexpected things out of the blue. We generally attribute those things to Murphy's Law. Good old Murph; he sure likes to wreak havoc whenever and wherever he can. Nonetheless, we hang in there. It is no different in our prayer life; as we get closer to a resolution in major issues, things come against us. That is the time to get more intensely involved in your prayer life and relationship to God. That is not the time to throw in the towel.

As a word of caution, lest you take what I've said the wrong way. Getting and staying ultimately involved in the process does not mean forgetting or relinquishing your existing responsibilities. It's much like the Parable of the Talents. (Matthew 25:14ff) We cannot bury what has been entrusted to us, otherwise we can lose that too. It is a dual responsibility that we have, vertically to our Lord and horizontally to the obligations in our everyday lives. So get up early, stay up late, find a place of solitude during your lunch break - be a guerrilla in your approach to God so that you can fulfill the dreams you have which will be blessed by Him. You can, and must be faithful, not only to Him but to your present responsibilities. God will move you in whatever direction is necessary when the time is right, when you can accept the change and YOU WILL KNOW IT! As a general rule God never takes you from one place without it being to another; even if you don't know up front specifically where it is. He will grant you grace to believe if you have taken the steps to be in touch. While you may be going in Faith you will have an idea where. This idea is continually expressed and expanded upon in the Book of Exodus as we see God leading the children of Israel throughout their journey to the Promised Land. The people of Israel were always under attack during the journey to their destination. Yet, as we know they did survive their ordeal, but they had to fight continuously. You may be surprised how well you can do what you're called upon to do daily when you spend time in guerrilla warfare. If you want to know God's will and direction for your life, know this; that if you're faithful today then you will be doing God's Will tomorrow, next week, next month, five years from now.

As I indicated earlier, my wife often exhorts me as the one who needs to do battle for our family. She maintains that I need to beg, plead and exhort with the Lord to move us forward. When she first came to me with this word of knowledge I looked at her as if she were crazy; after all our relationship to God is personal and we all have a responsibility. Then I realized that she viewed our situation much like I did, only she put it words that anybody can readily understand - It's not only a jungle out there, it also a battle. God is on our side but we need his help as well as being personally proactive in the battle. While it's true that God can do anything He wants to, whenever He wants to, it is also true that He uses people. And it may be YOU that He wants to enlist NOW; before your battle begins.

So what is it about war that drives everybody crazy? Why do we avoid the fact that there is a spiritual warfare going on all around us? Are we so self absorbed that we think God just does, even though we show no interest? In war, any kind of war, people die, people are injured (some for life); if the physical injuries go away psychological wounds oftentimes remain. In real life we are always affected by the tragedies that wars bring into the lives of people and we usually go out of our way to ensure that innocent bystanders are not affected any more than necessary. It's the same with spiritual warfare. We need to do all we can to make sure that our actions, or inactions, do not create any more fall out than absolutely necessary. Apologies after the fact, statements that we didn't mean to hurt you, etc. do not take away the hurt, they do not remove the barriers that we helped erect.

I remember when I built my first retirement housing project in Texas. My partners and I had a contract with the prime contractor, for a cost not to exceed. We had confidence in the man and the contract. So we gave him the plans and essentially said, (at least in our minds), call us when it's done and we'll come pick up the keys. It seemed reasonable to us at the time, until my banker summoned me to her office one day and quietly suggested that things were not going all that well at the construction site and that maybe someone in our group might want to take a personal interest in our project. What a rebuke! Here I thought that I was interested; after all I had secured the deal with an iron clad contract. I was totally ready. Boy, did I have a wrong number! The problem that faces us is that we cannot assume anything. We need to be involved in all of the details of our lives, not just the big picture; from the most important down to the minutest of details. Sometimes what seems least important comes back to haunt us if we leave it to chance.

In our spiritual walk it is the same thing. Our God is who can do whatever He wants, whenever He wants, but He does want to see what kind of personal interest we take in our relationship with Him. As my contract with the builder was guaranteed so is my eternal salvation guaranteed; I know that just like I knew that I would get the keys to my facility one day. The trip, however, is always fraught with problems, but should be fun, exciting and challenging and it will have infinitely more value and appeal if I'm involved with the details along the way.

We have a tendency at times to differentiate between our physical lives and our spiritual lives. Wrong! Our western mind set, coupled with Greek thought, has actually created a sort of dualism in Christianity; at least to the point of us working out our Christian faith. Additionally, ideas such as those postulated by Martin Luther, i.e., we have one foot in heaven and one foot on earth have further obfuscated the reality of the Christian life. In actuality, Luther's notion does not reflect a dualism but is rather more indicative of the truth. We do in fact live in two worlds; the world of the present, the here and now; and our hopes and thoughts are directed towards the next life, in heaven, which in one sense is to come and yet because it is in the spiritual realm, the fourth dimension, is here already, Because we give so much credence to our three-dimensional physical world we de-emphasize the spiritual world which is all around us. By not understanding the concept that our world is really more than what we see, feel, hear, smell and touch we have a tendency to make anything other than that a separate part of our life; a distinct part which has no relationship to the physical world around us.

I am no philosopher in the sense that I have philosophical credentials that would make me equal to those pedigreed dons in our institutions of higher learning. On the other hand I believe that I have grasped the sense whereof Scripture speaks. Ours is not just a world of concrete, nor is it just a world of flesh and bones, nor is it just water or any other matter. It is a world that is impacted and immersed in another dimension which we have chosen to ignore but which Scripture clearly tells us is there. *The spiritual realm.*

While you don't have to be a rocket scientist to sense the wholeness of God's creation, you do have to apply some common sense when viewing the completeness of God's creation. On the one hand we should stand in awe, if only because the very notion that the seen and the unseen are really one and the same, that both are necessary to make the whole. On the other hand we have been given the power to bridge the gap between the two worlds. Namely, the Holy Spirit, the one who opened the eyes of the prophets servant so that he could see the armies of the Lord protecting the city. Consequently, we need to recognize and live in both the physical world and the spiritual world, simultaneously. And when we do not do that we become part of the problem rather than part of the solution.

You see, you really can't have two personas; one for home and church, or work and church. It just doesn't work that way. Now many people refer to these dichotomies as being hypocritical but I reject that argument on the basis that you can't be hypocritical if you do not understand the basis of what you're saying. Hypocrisy is saying one thing while doing another; maintaining one thing while outwardly espousing a contradictory viewpoint. Too many people are so superficial in their thinking that they are classified as hypocrites. The difficulty that I see really is found in the dualism that we've talked about; either you see people that are so focused on the spiritual aspect of life that they have no conception of the real world, or you see people who acknowledge their faith but get so caught up in the struggle of everyday life that they miss out on what's really going on around them. The issue as I see it is that both groups are wrong in the sense that they have abdicated their responsibilities in the other area. They need to move to achieve a sense of balance. If anything, the title hypocrite should be attached to those Believers who should, due to the alleged influence of the Holy Spirit, be able to recognize that he/she needs to be in the world as well as in their spiritual mind.

The difficulty with dualism as we practice it in America, in our Christian churches, is that we have developed split personalities. We have a personality at home, a personality at work and a personality at church. After a while you can see where difficulties might occur. It doesn't take long before we forget to change hats in situations, and bingo, we're in trouble. And we're so cool, you know! We think for some reason that God also has a split personality, and that He views work as work, play as play, church as church, and so on. Our superb human reasoning dictates to us that if we avoid thinking about God then He doesn't see it. Because, you see, unless God happens to have his earth hat on while we're functioning in our earthly mode, then He going to miss what's going on.

If we understand the principle of guerrilla warfare, we know that there is a war going on. And this war is ongoing! The war is never over as long as we're on this earth. In many ways this is parallel in thought to the war that the United States fought in Vietnam, where a major problem was that American soldiers many times did not know who the enemy was or where they were. As a result it was difficult to fight a war when you didn't know who you were fighting. There has been, and still is a spiritual war being waged where we don't see the enemy but know he's there. As a result we must not only be on guard, but we must be decisive and proactive; not on the defensive but on the offensive. As believers we have saved our offense for the world and relegated our defense to our Christian walk. It's time that we not only put our worlds back together, the physical and the spiritual, but also our strategies, the defense and the offense. Our Christian mentality has always seemed to be that a good defense allows for a good offense. Unfortunately, it really is the opposite for believers. A good offense is the only defense we have. Matthew 11:12 - *Forceful men lay hold of the Kingdom.* We are not defense minded but offense minded. Be forceful! Be practical! Be shrewd as serpents! Be as innocent as doves! And as you open the gates of heaven His blessings will fall on you. More importantly, you will lead a balanced life, both in the physical realm and the spiritual. Yes, you can hasten the time it takes to get your prayers answered and you do so by being forceful, decisive and disciplined.

By recognizing that whether you like it or not, you really live in a multidimensional world in which it is your responsibility to live in harmony. But, more importantly, it is a multidimensional world in which you have available all the power and resources necessary to bring it into balance.

Maybe, that's what the Gospel is all about, a question of balance. Maybe we've focused so long on the preaching of the Gospel of Repentance that we've missed the point of the Gospel, namely the reconciliation of God to man and man to God. And that by missing the point we have missed the opportunity to incorporate the power of the spiritual world into our lives which is there for our taking; appropriating it into the physical world so that we can live harmoniously with God and each other. Think about it. Like everything else in life, it really is a matter of the Will! Yes we do live in a jungle. But it can be tamed because it already has been through Christ Jesus our Lord. We can win the war because in one sense it has already been won. Yet, as actors, as players on the eternal scene we have our battles that we must fight, both in the physical realm and in the spiritual realm. There is no future without going through the fires of life. It is not simply a matter of being like an ostrich and sticking our heads in the sand. In that case we only get wounded but we still have to move forward as soldiers. To that extent, then, why not start out right the first time, it may certainly be less ugly and will almost certainly be more positive.

CHAPTER EIGHT

EFFICIENCY VERSUS EFFECTIVENESS

O ur world rewards efficiency. If it looks good, feels good, tastes good and is available NOW, then it must be good. We are caught up in the NOW syndrome and we continuously try to polarize the NOW by making it appeal to and please all the senses. We are surrounded by this mentality. Nothing is done for the long haul, everything is done for today. Now, I do understand that biblically we can get caught up in this thought process, even though we oftentimes do so incorrectly. In Matthew 6:25 it says that *we should not be concerned about tomorrow;* some translations use the word worry. Unfortunately, we contextually miss the point here. While we are not to worry about tomorrow nowhere does it say that we shouldn't be prepared, that we shouldn't think about issues and situations.

Nowhere do I read that our spiritual forefathers were not prepared. After all, Moses spent 80 years preparing for his mission - 40 years at the court of Pharaoh and 40 years in the back side of the desert. In I Samuel we see how Samuel prior to his hearing the voice of God (even though he was called at young age) was being prepared under the guidance of Eli. In Acts 22:3 we note that Paul, prior to his conversion experience was trained under the tutelage of the preeminent scholar of the day, Gamaliel. At that time the learning process for young rabbis was extremely intense, the commitment to excellence being manifest in the lives of the students.

Frankly, I could go on. The difficulty with going on is that is not the heart of the issue. The issue is that believers today don't want to be prepared; they don't want to be disciplined nor do they want to engage in any kind of activity that requires work. Unfortunately, we have long recognized that those things important to us require work and discipline; relationships, your job, your marriage, your family, your softball game and even your bowling game - whatever. When it comes to fun things, we have no difficulty spending hours honing and practicing our skills. We have also finally decided, at least some have, that time spent in cultivating relationships requires work so we get counseling or do whatever to develop those skills. But, when it comes to our Faith it is another story. We somehow think that, through osmosis or some other exotic means, we are going to somehow know and understand all things, that we are going to be expert in all things NOW and, by cracky, nobody is going to violate our right to be right, even if we don't have a clue.

It's all in the packaging, at least that's what the Madison Avenue gurus keep telling us. And we've applied that mentality to our Christian lives. Hence, our feeling has become one that if we say the right things (remember, Christians have a language all their own, developed over centuries of careful refinement] then we must be right. So we dress up for the occasion, pick up on what someone has flippantly zeroed in on and presto, we are available, refined, purposeful, holy, prophets of God. The preparation time has been a big zilch but boy we're experts. Now, we go out and lay it on the brethren - from God, naturally. We are so efficient in presenting the message, the Word! And when we speak, the pastor or some other respected church leader confirms what we've said and it is now sealed in the archives of heaven. Boy are we locked into the Kingdom now.

Additionally we get much of our confirmation from all the Christian Radio and Television that we expose ourselves to. Never before have I seen as much confusion caused by a medium as I have from Christian Radio and Television. As I listen to or watch, I am amazed at the indoctrination proffered by this medium. There is, in my opinion, very little differentiation between the secular and religious electronic media. Both offer, that thinking should be left to someone other than us. Apparently the average Christian is good only for reaction and acceptance. preferably acceptance only. And the messages that come across the airwaves, from program to program, is oftentimes even more confusing. Let me give you an example. One TV pastor says that we must have faith or we will never achieve our goals or dreams. Another one will say that faith must be added to the measure of doing something while a third will postulate that doing something is valid only through the giving process, preferably to that ministry as that is where you heard it first. And this goes on and on! Three messages, the same yet different. Supposedly all truth, yet different. What is the distinction here and who makes this distinction? Probably a fourth interpretation. In many ways what is happening here is reflective of what Paul talks about in II Timothy 4:3-4, . . . *to suit their own desires, they will gather around them a great number of teachers to say what their itching ears want to hear.*

We can hear anything that we want to hear these days. We have been duped into believing that our self selected religious leaders have the only real answers. And if we don't hear it from our pastor we will get if from some TV pastor. Whatever we want to hear! If we wait long enough, or do sufficient channel surfing, we will hear it, to confirm what it is we want to hear. In this sense then we really do live in a world that Marshall McLuhan so aptly wrote about in the 60's, *the medium really is the message* ... as well as the massage for our lives. If it's on TV or radio, then it must be right. We have lost our ability to think critically and, more importantly, we not only let others think for us but pay them to do so. And then to add insult to injury, we let these people intimidate us into believing that any criticism of them is of the devil. They are right and what they say is of God; therefore, if we say anything against them it must be from Satan, and it is now we who are at fault and we are the ones who are made to feel guilty. Good job guys! No wonder, a world that is going to hell in a hand basket has little regard for the message, the good news, the gospel.

Now I have a very simple approach to the issues of life's questions and seeming inconsistencies. The first approach comes from my understanding of Scripture where I note in I Corinthians 14:33 that *our God is not the author of disorder or confusion.* Secondly, as my philosophy professor in graduate school so aptly reminded us, that in our search for truth we must always remember that truth, when mingled with error (no matter how small the error might be) is no longer truth but is now a new error. Our world, our philosophical bent for truth has become a mishmash of conflicting signals and suggestions that obscure than reveal, that confuse rather than enlighten, that cover up rather than uncover. To that extent I have concluded that the only solution is for me to become more interested and concerned with consistency in the preaching of the Gospel and that de facto agreement with everything that I hear, see or read is doing a tremendous injustice to our Lord, the Christian community at-large and to me.

Is there no one who will stand up and say enough already! A pastor of a large church once said that he could handle any kind of criticism regarding his leadership, etc. but that the lay person was to stay out of his preaching as that was sacred. (Actually, he didn't say it once, it was a theme of his ministry). In these situations I reminded of what Shakespeare wrote so long ago, *me thinks thou doest protest too much.* Now I may appear real picky here but I do want to make a point! This individual was (is) a marvelous individual; a godly man, I believe. It appears to me that he generally has his ear inclined to God. Nonetheless, many of his sermons were filled with misleading biblical inaccuracies, whether misquotes, misleading application of Scripture, total misuse of the English language, etc. Now, if I don't feel that I can tell a man of his inaccuracies in the pulpit, how can he correct any of his mistakes? Will he? Shouldn't he be accurate in his usage of words and grammar, so that people aren't misled and further confused? Can he expect (or should he expect) that everyone will recognize his errors for what they are and that people will zero in on the intent of his message? I think not! It is evident that the average Christian is more sheep than he/she will admit. As a result Martin Luther's main thesis of *the individual priesthood* of the believer is not only forgotten but that responsibility has been handed over to a new priestly tribe, namely preachers, evangelists, etc. who do not speak with a consistent voice, who obfuscate by delivering nothing more than noise, who are oftentimes more interested in their own ego gratification than speaking and doing what is right. And if you, in the midst of this cauldron of clanging cymbals and noise, have the audacity to criticize in any form or fashion then it is highly recommended that you find another place of worship. One such individual, on TV, had the gall to publicly postulate that he refused to have people in his church who didn't agree with what he said. Excuse me! Is it your church or God's church? Who elected you God? I believe that the Pope around Martin Luther's time had a similar opinion of criticism. It is past time for the community of believers to march forward, in soldierly fashion to reclaim the gospel.

There is no question that modern technology allows for the gospel to be preached in a more efficient manner. And in many cases it does so very effectively but the concept of the word effectively has changed to reflect self glory for the preacher and his ministry rather than for that of our Lord. In his book, "A World without Heroes" George Roche reminds us that we cannot be too precise when we articulate the truth, and we as hearers of the Word have the responsibility to differentiate between truth and error, even if our (self appointed) leaders do not seem to want to do so. The packaging! We have gotten so used to responding to the packaging that we have forgotten about the package. And when we finally do get to the package itself we have no comprehension about what's inside. The wrapping has titillated our senses to the point that we no longer care about the package, only the pretty wrapping. I blame our religious leaders for that. During my youth, the pastor of the little church I attended was such an authoritarian, such a myopic individual, that I wanted to worship anywhere but there. That was not my concept of God, as He had revealed himself to me. Then as I matured I looked for a God who really cared, about me, not just for eternity but for here, now. And out of this milieu has grown a movement that is affected by what tickles the ears. Isn't it time that we took responsibility for our own walk with God? The time has come to make our lives more than a three-dimensional experience but rather a four dimensional one. The two dimensional quality of electronic religion is out of touch with the reality that wants to touch all of us. We certainly have become very efficient in the presentation over the past decades but the effectiveness of the presentation has become lost in the form. The function has been replaced by the form and today we wander aimlessly in a labyrinth of confusion and uncertainty while we have a God who says you have certainty if you only place your trust in me. And in the blur of the modern evangelism and doctrinal propaganda we have lost the main import of the Gospel, namely that God became man, and died for man, and rose again so that fellowship would be restored, not just for the next life but for here and for now. There is nothing in Scripture that maintains that today is sacrificed for tomorrow, that the needs and hurts of today are sublimated for the next life. The only thing that Scripture maintains is that *we are to become a whole being, physically and spiritually. Yes, we have become effectively efficient in promoting the Gospel but what Gospel is it?*

CHAPTER NINE

FREEDOM VERSUS LIBERATION

We are, as previously discussed, certainly a NOW generation. Everything is to be apprehended and comprehended NOW. If it doesn't happen, NOW it is time to move on. After all, we have the freedom to make those choices. We are a liberated people. So, if God doesn't answer this prayer NOW, it must be the format of the prayer that is the root of the problem. Therefore, I will find a new format, a new, more powerful formula. And we are never satisfied until we find a formula that works. This new approach to religious rapprochement smacks of a Hegelian philosophy that ultimately led to Marxism and we know where that ultimately led.

I once had a business partner whose main locus in thinking was symptomatic of this syndrome. I don't know why, maybe it was his legal training, but if something didn't work right away, like several days then it had to be scrapped for something different. The impatience of the man was incredible and drove me batty. The dollars that were indiscriminately spent to find a NOW answer drove me nuts. Now, don't get me wrong here, it is important to get off a track that is going nowhere. On the other hand, bailing out at the first sign of difficulty is also a problem. If we've gone through the process of thinking and praying through the options, we should have a little more discipline than that. I am reminded of the People of Israel, on the way to the Promised Land. We know what kind of bailing out they did. Bad news, it ticked God off real bad.

If we think through issues, meditate on them and prayerfully consider them, then we should be clear on where we're heading. After all, the decision was hopefully one done in concert with the leading of God. Will we never make a mistake, even using this concept, of course not? Sometimes we will. Will we ever change our course? Hopefully! God has given us this freedom to engage the decision we elect. We are free to jump ship at any time just as we are free to jump on board at any time.

Freedom is an interesting concept, especially in America. In one sense our concept of freedom is what attracts people from all over the world. In another sense it gives us massive headaches. In this country we can pretty much think, do and say what we want. Well think and say, anyway! The doing part is subjective in that there are so many governmental and judicial regulations that many times we are hamstrung. This is especially true in business. Try doing business with the government some time and you will see what I mean. The red tape is enough to discourage even the hardiest of people. The general populace doesn't know much about government interference in the ordinary activities of men primarily because most people either do not care nor they do not operate in a sphere where they encounter this stifling interference.

In the realm of personal freedom it is a little different. Because our society is so tolerant it is easy to pretty much do, think and say what you want and as long as you stay within the generally perceived bounds created by our laws you're pretty much O.K. Yet there is an evident sense of frustration. It is becoming obvious that whenever we venture out of our self-imposed cocoon that we are fair game for everyone or anything. It seems that we oftentimes build our own walls. We isolate ourselves at home, with friends, at work, at church, with our family, whatever. For many of us life has become single dimensional. While our world in general has shrunk and is still shrinking our private worlds are also becoming smaller. Not only have we become afraid of issues such as crime we have become prisoners of our thought process. We don't like to go out because the crowds at the mall are too big. We don't want to go out because the lines are too long. We don't want to go to church on Sunday nights because we get home too late. We don't want to live in such or such a neighborhood because the homes are too old. We don't visit friends because the traffic is too heavy. We don't participate in civic responsibilities because the required energy is too much. After all, we gave at work or at home. The TV calls us to linger and vegetate. It's easier to be an observer to life than a participant.

So we build our walls and these walls soon extend out to every aspect our lives, including our spiritual life and it is this aspect that I want to talk about. I'll leave the balance to the sociologists even though those external issues affect us Christians even more than we realize. And I attribute that to what I call the *dysfunctional Christian syndrome*. All too often we hear of issues arising in a person's life that were really caused by issues arising out of the process of growing up . . . physical, mental, sexual abuse, whatever. Much of this mentality has arisen this century, out of the development of modern psychology. And while this modern psychology has created a world of seekers who look for someone to give them answers, the syndrome for Christians is pretty much the same. Everybody, wants to be counseled to the extent that they can be absolved of responsibility, so that they can escape a meaningful and personal response to life.

As I was growing up, I was impacted by an old world *churchology*. Everything was bad, including me. The rules and regulations were tough and adhering to them certainly took the fun out of life. Yet, the freedom allowed to me by the world was incredible. As a result the confusion arising from apparent contradictions was immense. Let me try to explain without offending you. Nowhere in Scripture is there a black and white admonition against alcohol. In fact, the argument that wine is good for a person was made by the apostle Paul in his writing to Timothy. (I Timothy 5:23) Yet many good people in conservative evangelical churches make this an issue of fellowship. Not necessarily based on sound doctrine but rather on dogmatic principles. I grew up in a very conservative German Baptist church where beer and wine were the order of the day, especially after church on Sundays. Imagine my consternation and confusion the first time I set foot in a Southern Baptist church! That's the way it is so often in our churches. One has an issue with this and the other an issue with something else, and so and so forth. Issues that are not specifically addressed in Scripture have become dogmatic rules for many churches. A good example of this is the question of celibacy for priests in the Roman Catholic Church. When one adds to these thematic aberrations that the churches have adopted over the centuries a generation of why askers or prove to me individuals a major problem occurs especially when the ensuing because or because I say so answers leave one totally out in the cold. The response doesn't fit, the response doesn't answer the question so the new generation goes elsewhere. To some extent then, the new generation adopts a *non-theistical attitude*. Furthermore, coupled with the ever increasing laxity of morals within our society the non-answers postulated by the Church become increasingly more irrelevant. Then we are confronted with the freedom as espoused in Scripture (what preachers say, not what we can do) in addition to the freedoms of our land and presto we have a nice, neat dysfunctional world. In my judgment it is this contradictory teaching, publicly and in our churches, that creates an environment whereby generally good people feel that they are within their rights as believers to go out and kill doctors who perform abortions. It is amazing that we have come so far and yet regressed so much.

So we have developed a dysfunctional Christian family and the disparate demands on this family, from both church and society, create individuals who do not know what they believe, what they should believe and what they can believe. More importantly we don't teach these people how to think - period! As a result we give up our freedom to think to anyone who tells us what to think; this can be our pastor, the TV evangelist(s), you name it. They appeal to our emotions and our feelings, not to our ability to logically reason. Their very approach to the Gospel denies the basic approach of an apostle no less in stature than the Apostle Paul who used logic and reason to persuade; he did not discourage thinking but capitalized on the ability of reason to change lives. If faith is a function of the will (as is suggested in Romans 12:2 where it says that . . . *the renewing of the mind and God's will* go hand in hand, then I believe that the average, modern Christian has generally abdicated his mind and hence his ability to practice sound judgment. The only people who apparently demonstrate that they have a mind are our so-called Christian leaders and it has become painfully evident that many of them have no mind at all as they preach only rules and regulations; your modern day scribes and Pharisees, if you will. At the same time many others demonstrate a capacity for capitalizing on new thoughts and processes inconsistent with Scripture, while doing nothing more than building up egos and coffers. As I write this I think of the successful TV evangelist types who, after getting you emotionally fired up, say write to me. I want to hear from you. Let me know that I'm getting through to you! I'd like to meet someone some day who actually got through to one of these guys and was able to really visit with him or actually get a personal letter, not a form letter, response number 23 for this type request.

I perceive our attitude in this case much like I do professional sports or entertainment. We complain about the money that athletes and movie stars make and further complain about how inconsequential their efforts are, or how they let us down as role models or whatever. Yet we still pay to see them play. We still go to the movies. We still elect the same people to government and we still let the same religious leaders bamboozle us with half-baked truths. We let these guys appeal to our emotions, only to leave us high and dry because so often our prayers are not answered, our dreams are not realized but yet the guilt is showered upon us. If the Bible is a *How to* Book and if God is a *How to* God, then why aren't our preachers down where we live, in our face type individuals who minister about the powers of the almighty? Elijah was, as was Elisha. Isaiah was. What gives here, anyway? Take back your faith, your ability to commune with God. You want answers? I've got a deal for you, but YOU have to do it! You have the brains, the power, the time (even if it's in the wee hours of the morning while everybody else is sleeping or perish the thought, if it has to be a night while everyone else is watching the Late Show). Here's the gig! Take out your Bible, get a good concordance (find some resources that explain Scripture properly). There are many tools, many sound interpretations of Scripture that are faithful to the original. Begin to read. Make it a plan to read the Bible through from cover to cover. Begin to learn who God is. Begin to develop your own personal relationship. Then bring the rest of your family into what is happening in your life. Need Help? Dial 1-800-ASK-GOD. It's a toll-free call. It's never busy. And He always talks to you personally, as if you were the only one he was talking to. Recapture the freedom that you gave up to others. You don't have to be afraid. You're liberated! You are free, if you want to be. The Reformation, as initiated by Luther, Zwingli and others gave us the tools to be free, so why then have we abrogated these right, this responsibility, this opportunity?

I pause here to say a word of caution. As Romans 12:2 suggests, our Christian walk is a process, a learning process at that. You will make mistakes, count on it. If you misread direction from God, He will correct you, if you seek His help. Challenge those who teach you. I've noted one thing over the years; there are very few apostle Paul types who have it all together. Don't be confused between style and substance. Just because your preacher has some style and apparently no substance does not mean that you toss him out, or go elsewhere, unless, of course, after some time you determine he's totally nuts. You continuously search for truth, for reality, for substance. Remember, no one walks in your shoes except you. The little church that we presently attend is an example of what I'm talking about. It's primarily a blue collar congregation that seems to be majoring on form rather than function; needs are addressed by bringing everything out in the open as opposed to a consistent, practical, biblically based preaching and teaching. While it doesn't do much for me in one sense, I do meet God there, consistently; in fact it was Sunday, August 21, 1994 while meeting with God, that resulted in this book. While the pastor never seems to hit or touch on the reality I need, I do love his spirit and I meet God. And God talks to me. He encourages me. He provides for me. He answers me. He allows me to bring down the walls. But as I observe what is happening to people here, I note that they stay fixed on what the pastor says, not necessarily on God's leading.

Do you want your life back? Your future? Your today? Be a guerrilla. It's not just enough to be a soldier in God's army. Fight the fight to survive. *Be as shrewd as a serpent but as innocent as a dove.* Remember the enemy can read too. He knows the plan - probably better than you. My wife put it quite aptly to me some time ago; wives have a way of getting to the heart of a matter and if we men would listen more and not always get defensive we might learn something. She told me that if we, as a family, were going to move forward that I had to fight for our family. That I had to do whatever it takes to win the war. If you want to win, do what it takes. Be a warrior, be a guerrilla.

Sometimes, our society's fixation with winning is counterproductive and we have become desensitized to the concept of what winning entails. Even Paul admonished us to run reach race in a winning matter. In this case, however, we need to understand that our freedom, our liberation is contingent on us winning the war. Our individual battle is with the forces that strive to keep us down. Sitting back and doing nothing, placing the total burden on God really is counterproductive and does nothing but rob us of our victory. Our freedom, our liberation stems from living in the source of our victory, Jesus, not in the confines of walls which restrict rather than open. Iron bars do not a prison make!

CHAPTER TEN

CHURCH AS BUSINESS

It appears to me that very few people believe that the modern church is solely a spiritual body anymore. As I traverse through life I hear, more and more, that individuals are turned off by the big business image that many churches present. And if it's not a big business image, because most churches certainly are small, then it's just the basic notion that churches are after only one thing, namely money. Additionally, when one adds para-church organizations and media ministries to the equation and perceive that they gather a disproportionate number of adherents then the big business concept becomes evident... and rightfully so!

There is no question that any organization, just as individuals, needs finances to operate. To perform its mission statement, a church or any other religious organization needs cash. I don't think that anyone would argue that cash becomes an essential, if not the essential ingredient to make things work in this technological age. Fund raising is a messy affair and certainly is not for the faint of heart. The fact that it takes a certain type of individual to successfully raise money may be a problem in itself when we talk about the church. The difficulty around church finances revolves around the methods used to acquire this cash and the accountability associated with it. It is in this area that we see so much disparity today.

In my early years in business I had a mentor who made a point that has stayed with me for well over 25 years now; *perception is* reality. It doesn't matter *if you're doing the job well* what matters is if people perceive you doing the job well. While I would not necessarily say that I like this concept I have found that it is a true statement as far as generalizations go. People don't care if you're working your fingers to the bone if the three times they see you, all you're doing is goofing off, the general impression here being that is what you do all the time. Once that image is planted in somebody's mind it is extremely difficult to change. Interestingly enough the church, along with related ministries, does a poor job in this area. In fact most churches don't even try to deal with this issue of perception. In fact, if anything, most pastors deal with this issue by defensively pointing the finger at the laity by simply saying that they (the laity) don't give enough. Others simply don't talk about finances, believing, like an ostrich, that if they avoid talking about that it will go away. Others just become belligerent and put people on a guilt trip.

As a believer I have had the opportunity to deal with this issue both from an insider and outsider role. I've been both an executive pastor, where a prime responsibility has been the financial business of the church. Additionally I've been on church finance committees so I do have a little experience in this area and it is really generally not a pretty picture. All too often I see where the average lay person is completely bamboozled, befuddled and down right lied to by groups who reject the basic notion of accountability. It's almost as if they believe that knowledge will somehow eradicate programs. One mustn't give too much information lest people develop an understanding. And if a person questions, then the person asking has the problem, it certainly isn't in the area of presentation. And the bottom line is that too many churches have abrogated responsibility in this area to the pastor who, as a man of God, is oftentimes the least equipped person to have anything to do with issues such as finances. The church, in many ways, operates like our political system, with one major distinction. At least politicians can be voted out of office, whereas the average leader of a church has God (and His Will) as a final court of last appeal, even if the logic behind the reasoning borders on the absurd. You'd be surprised as to how many people buy into that concept.

Some churches do try to be financially accountable. They prepare detailed budgets and regularly report back to the church body. Some never ask for money and do extremely well. I was chief operating officer of such a church once, where the offering plate was never passed, where people wanted to give regularly and where they gave more than what was required. Even when we were without a pastor for several years, the programs went on, the giver kept on giving. The budget even went up. This was due primarily to a pastor who educated his people to what was biblically required of them, trained them in how to be good stewards, *gave them* good information as to what was going on, and let them make the financial decisions. This kind of church is unquestionably the exception to the rule. Most churches, unfortunately, operate like our Government - Here's the number, leave the details to us. Then the guilt trip begins! We need money, programs can't go on. But nobody seems to know where the funds have gone. And if you ask, then you are not demonstrating faith in the leadership. At that point you'd best leave before you're asked to leave.

And much of this problem is caused by the control aspect of pastor's egos. Surrounding themselves with yes men these individuals leave no room for doing a job properly. All that these individuals want is to look good. They want to cultivate perception all right, the perception of their purity as men of God. I recall an article in a sporting magazine one time where football players were being interviewed regarding their perception of themselves and their roles as players. There was a rather interesting insight presented by the large contingent of black players who were interviewed. Many of them indicated that it wasn't always making the big play that counted. If that wasn't possible, if they messed up, or failed to make a big play, then it was of primary importance *that they looked good failing.* Pastors oftentimes present a similar image to their parishioners and in context of letting the pastor look good, many church members struggle with their own difficulties in making it through life. As believers, whether clergy or lay person, we're not called to *look good, we're called to be faithful and obedient.* Looking good is not our responsibility, it's God's!

Celluloid ministries are even better than churches in this regard. In church you at least see live bodies. Celluloid ministers cajole you into sending money to a pristine looking organization that has nothing better to do than build fancy houses, drive expensive cars and send out four color magazines that extol the virtues of what God is doing in the ministry. It is because of the deceit and deception of many of these ministries in recent years that I have concluded that it is wrong for us to send money directly to these organizations. I'm not saying that many don't deserve our support but I don't believe they should be supported directly. In my judgment, if a celluloid ministry should be supported, it should be done through the local church. I don't know what it is about these celluloid ministries that attracts so much attention. They never seem to have difficulty getting volunteers to work, and it seems that 90% of their time is spent soliciting money. There's something wrong when the local church suffers (albeit perhaps because they created their own dilemma) while two dimensional, celluloid organizations appear to be highly successful. If giving to these groups would be through the local church then we might see a reporting and accountability process built into the system.

I am a firm believer that all financial giving should be through the local church. The local church is still the vehicle that God uses to ensure that his plan is implemented. Make sure your church has a system set up for accountability, that you know where you are and where you're headed. Then, as worthy ministries come up that require funds the church can decide to support them. It's all up front and the church body agrees to support a worthwhile enterprise. Frankly, while this approach would put a number of celluloid ministries out of business, those that were genuine would do even better than present and they would have the support of local churches rather than being a spiritually divisive medium.

This is a rather difficult concept to get across because nobody wants to admit that their pet charity is exactly that, a pet charity. Only when we recognize our real responsibility, to God and to His church, will we ever move forward. At the same time we do not leave ultimate the accountability of our church to chance. We actively participate in the process, knowing what's going on and how it's happening. Your finances to the church are important. Remember that! But, at the same time, remember that you do not abdicate your responsibilities just because you give, you take on more. This is especially true when so many believers really do sacrifice in their giving. So many give their last mite and place their trust in individuals who have not nearly the depth of faith and commitment that poor individuals have. It really is a travesty and an injustice.

So, in your quest for the perfect place of worship, your place of service, check it out first. What checks and balances are there in place? Don't blindly accept that all is good because the praise and worship service makes you feel good, yet when you want to get involved you are really no more than a necessary nuisance for some individuals who have other agendas. So rather than get upset when you're being taken for a ride, be proactive in advocating for change, or if that is not possible then find a place where perception and reality really do meet. That's not to say that you're going to find perfection in any local body. Unfortunately, churches are comprised of people, and even as believers we're *not perfect, only being perfected.* But you can ask questions, you can make suggestions, you can be involved. So, if you're not involved in all aspects then don't belly ache when you don't like what you see. You do have a choice and the choice begins with you being a good steward. Being a good steward does not just mean money, but means time, energy and the willingness to be more than just a sheep.

While Jesus frequently made the reference to humans as being sheep I am convinced that this was not because we are sheep but because we behave like sheep, especially in spiritual matters. If you stop to think about what being a sheep really means, then you will do your utmost to change your world view and become the adopted son or daughter of God that you have been called to be.

CHAPTER ELEVEN

PLATEAUS . . . OR UPS AND DOWNS, AND UPS AGAIN.

I don't know about you but I oftentimes get frustrated about my lack of progress in both my spiritual life as well as everyday living. I combine the two because I'm really not as good in compartmentalizing these two aspects of my life as our society would deem appropriate. I used to be able to do a much better job of this but not anymore. My walk with the Lord needs to be a 24 hour, ongoing thing. Dualism, in the sense of modern compartmentalization, has no role in my life. I find that I no longer can shut off one area of my life and effectively deal with another.

Consequently, I tend to gauge personal progress on two planes - the three-dimensional world of the physical and the fourth dimensional world of the spiritual and it is essential that the two are in harmony. My personal frustration occurs when I look at those times when it was evident that the spiritual and physical dimensions of my life were in perfect harmony. Life in all its senses was good. Then there are those other times when my spiritual life as well as my everyday existence seemed to be removed from my being. How can this be? How do we reconcile this anomaly so that we don't go nuts? How can we go back to that time when everything seemed to be perfectly synchronized?

The religious individuals in our world, those modern day scribes and Pharisees, will tell us that it is obvious that we are the problem. It is we who have moved away from God. That it is because of sin in our life. In my judgment those accusations are not only oversimplifications but border on the heretical. There is only one accuser of the brethren and that is not another brother!

First, I do not dispute that we're all sinners, because we are. Second, I know that we can do things that disfellowship us from God and that we need to correct those problems and/or resolve any outstanding issues. Third, as previously discussed in another chapter, God does hear us when we earnestly seek him. We could go on and on but you get the point. Even when we bind Satan the problem still exists. So what is the real problem? Is it our unrealistic expectations? After all, isn't our Father the richest dude in the Universe? He can do and give whatever He wants, whenever He wants. Why do we feel that we're all over the place when it comes to reconciling our spiritual walk with life in general?

This phenomenon, that happens to every believer at some or another is what I call *regression* analysis. I must admit that this is treading new ground for me, and regression analysis in this sense has nothing to do with the statistical term that is used in academia. What I mean by regression analysis in this sense is as follows. *We human beings, always tend to hang our hats on the last major experience, positive or negative, with which we identify.* In my case it was a period, some time ago, where my spiritual walk was so tuned in to God that my outward walk was directly and immediately affected - positively. It was like I was getting specific *marching orders* on a regular basis. I really believe that is the key, where the spiritual directly translates us out of the third dimension into perfect harmony with the spiritual dimension. I'm not talking about a spiritual high here, one that you come down from after a period of worship. What I am talking about is a synchronization of all of the dimensions of life. The problem arises when we let the physical overtake the spiritual, when everyday problems and issues start to drive the train as opposed to being a part of the train.

When that happens, it doesn't take long to realize that we're not getting the same pizzazz out of our lives - in any form or fashion. At that point we begin to search for why so that we can go back to our last major reference point. And we do everything in our power to achieve that past harmony but it usually fails with the result being that we are even more frustrated because we can't go back to what we had. Where we're missing the boat is that we can never go back. That's what I'm referring to in my use of regression analysis. We're always looking behind us, trying to determine what worked for us back when, and how we did it. And because of this tendency we are missing what is in front of us.

The problem with staying where we're at is that is not reality. The Law of Entropy dictates *that left unto themselves, things will deteriorate.* Ergo, if we're not moving forward in our spiritual walk (and I'm talking about deliberately and cognitively) then we're going to get some slippage. The real question is how much slippage. Could it be a just a little, or have we slipped even past the point that we are trying to reference?

It has been my observation that Christians try to get to their previous reference point, not knowing which side they are on and hence become frustrated when no results are achieved. I am convinced that the solution to this is quite simple, so simple in fact that I missed it myself for a long time. When you're off track, then the only thing to do is get on track - Wherever, you're at. It is up to God to do the rest. The only person who cares where you got off the track is you and frankly, Satan, who loves to remind you that you messed up. Frankly, you'll drive yourself nuts trying to go back and getting on the track where you fell off. We spend too much time trying to figure out where we fell off and getting back to there that we are too long getting back on the track so we lose even more time. The bottom line is that it's as simple as Isaiah points out in Chapter 58, verse 9. *You will call for help and He will say here am I .* The upshot is not that God says call on me for help when you figure out where you're at, or call me when you know how you got to where you're at. You ask and God appears. Get back on the track where you're at. You use that as a starting point. You don't know what you missed since your falling off the track. The only thing you know is that God is talking to you now. Just get on the track, looking forward, and let God take care of the past, both good and bad.

Now you say, I've done that but there still is no reconciliation to my issue, my problem. Naturally, you're frustrated, but it is herein that the key to the resolution of the problem lies. You don't find the problem first and then get on track, you get on track first and then look for the root problems that are afflicting you. When that happens recognition and understanding will occur but you may not like the response. Be prepared to recognize that we still live in a world of cause and effect. We generally have to let the effects of what we were instrumental in causing run their due course. Once again, this doesn't mean that God can't or won't intervene but He may not. You may find yourself on track but needing to work through the consequences of those previous actions. It is this that I believe Jesus meant when he said that He will help you carry the burden because it is sometimes, those consequences that become unbearable but yet have to be carried if we are to remain on track.

In addition to cause and effect there is also what I call the *solicitation theory*. Anything that deals with getting us out of the jam we got ourselves into is *solicitous*. The most difficult thing to accomplish is to decipher between consequences and solicitation. Try to follow with me in the following example. You're out of work and you need a job. In the first place, God knows that you need a job, that you need to provide for the essentials of life such as food, shelter and clothing. The real question is why are you out of a job in the first place? The following represents only a partial litany of reasons why this may have happened to you: (1) You were fired. Why? Did you perform poorly? If so, how? Can you correct the underlying reasons? You may be experiencing the effects of something you helped cause. Find out what it is and then move on. (2) you were laid off. This one is not quite as simple. It's not always a numbers game; the economy can be blamed for only so much. Perhaps if you hadn't job hopped for so long, the seniority issue now affecting you would be a non issue. If it really was the economy, the cause and effect theory doesn't apply; now you are soliciting. (3) You quit. Why did you quit? Didn't like your boss, your co-workers, the work you were doing? This is by definition a cause and effect item. Unless you have a new job to go to it is your decision that got you here. Furthermore, if you left a job where there were previously unresolved issues, all you did was take those issues (issues that are now more deeply rooted) to the next job. Once again we have a situation of cause and effect. The problem really may not have been your job but something inherent in your personality, work ethic or whatever.

Most of the situations depicted above are generally related to some cause with related effect. The cause is generally something that you can control - you! All too often we engage mouth or walking shoes before we engage brain. Then we cry foul! Get on track and learn from what the Holy Spirit is trying to teach you and if you'll let him He will keep you from going under. Sometimes you may only receive enough to get by on - maybe just day by day. But then when that happens we get fixated on the problem not on the solution (which is in us) and then we get mad at God, only we couch it terms like nobody wants me, I'm a failure, etc. Wait a minute. If you're going to get mad at someone, be mad at yourself. God didn't create the problem, you did. But like any good parent He wants you to see where you're going, where you went wrong, so that you don't make the same mistake again and then be at the doorstep asking him to pull you out of the muck again and again. Then when He finally says enough, already and leaves you to your own devices which you have now demonstrated are your general methods of operation, we don't understand why His blessings don't fall on us. We're so ingrained in our own personality disorders that we couldn't recognize God if He literally came knocking at our door.

God told me one time that all of the elements were in place for me to solve my issues, receive his blessings and finally move on. I remember the day, it was clear as a bell. While I believed him, I still couldn't understand the wait principle. O.K. God, I heard you. Wonderful. Now let me have it. I'm ready. Whoops! I'm back off track, still not understanding that he expects me to work within the framework that has been created for me. Namely to honor the commitment to him! And to be diligent in maintaining and nurturing that commitment. Sometimes I'm still like a little kid and when I don't get that toy right away then the disappointment of the moment leads to daddy doesn't love me nor does he care. If you believe that God confirmed his word to you and that you received your answer, then test the spirits and move on in faith. You may need to go down the track a ways before you see the manifestation of his promise so it doesn't do you any good to get off track and stay there if you need to move forward does it? When you're on the track, move! If you don't, you may find yourself going backwards again.

Before I go on there is a verse that I need to share with you that talks about the disappointment issue addressed above. Maybe this will help you to understand God and how he really feels about you. In II Corinthians 5:15 we read *And he died for all, that those who live should live no longer live for themselves, but for him who died for them, and was raised again.* In and of itself this verse means very little to the average believer but it really has some significant value for us. In Old Testament times which then culminated with the death and resurrection of our Lord it was dictum that blood was used to cover the sins of the people. Needless to say our Lord did that for us when he died on the cross. However, a little regarded additional fact is actually more important here. In that part of the world it was, and in some cases still is, *custom* that when someone gives his life for someone else several things happen. First, the person who is still alive because another died for him, pledges eternal allegiance to the one who gave his life for him; if not to him because he is himself now dead then to the family because that is a debt that cannot ever be repaid. To that extent the person who still lives becomes a vassal or a slave to the dead person's memory and/or his family etc. Additionally, there is another thought here that is even more important than you or I becoming slaves to Jesus because he died for us. It is also custom in Semitic culture that if someone saves the life of another then he, from that moment on, takes full responsibility for the life of the person he saved. And it is to that end that we not only pledge our allegiance to our Lord Jesus but have the confidence that he NOW has the full responsibility for our lives . . . every detail thereof. So when you fret, when things are going badly, when you get angry or become disappointed, remember that Jesus has taken full responsibility for your life. And this applies not only for the future but also right now. So don't be mad at God. Get on your knees in thankful adoration that he is your protector, that he is your guide, that he is your provider. Ask him to open your eyes so that you may see. After all, like it or not he is responsible for you and he took on this responsibility because he loves you. So when you get down and depressed, thinking nobody cares about you or the issues you face keep this thought in mind; there is someone who has taken total responsibility for you and will demonstrate his love and concern if you'll just let him.

The final aspect in this section relates to something I call *experiential anxiety*. Sometimes we don't like to move forward because we don't know what the future holds - be it tomorrow, next week or a lifetime away. We are content in our present state, ergo nothing more needs to be done. We got the new job - be happy. That's great and I truly am happy for you but remember this one thing - if you stop along the track you may wind up going backwards or even getting run over and pushed off the track. But I'm happy where I'm at! Good, but your relationship with God still needs to move forward because we don't know what challenges and opportunities await us, in any aspect of our lives unless we stay plugged in. Remember, *to whom much has been given, much shall be demanded* , (Luke 12:48) So if you've moved up another notch on the spiritual ladder it is your responsibility to continuously check the spiritual thermometer with regards to your relationship to God. He has done, continues to do and will continue to do his part. Isn't it easier to just keep moving forward? Starting that train up again and again is an extremely laborious process. As we go along life's journey we keep adding cars of baggage and the train takes more and more time in getting up to speed after we stop. It takes so much energy that we really do get tired; we get spiritually and physically exhausted. It makes so much more sense to keep the train moving at all times; even if it's slow, it's better than stop and go. Keep moving forward. Don't be afraid of what's in front; I have it on good report that you'll like it. Rather than be afraid of what's in front, be afraid of sliding backwards, be afraid of getting run over if you stop. President Roosevelt once said *that the only thing we should fear is fear itself!* Now that's something to be afraid of! The scenery and the landscape and the blessings are all there; continuously.

We often hear that it's good to stop and smell the roses. I believe in that concept and no, it does not contradict what I just said. Smelling the roses along the way; or stopping and smelling any of God's creation, that which we are stewards over is part of the process. Sometimes people become such literalists that they miss the point. Enjoying, savoring, respecting and being thankful for what God has provided for us is not stopping in the normal sense. At this point we're talking about not a physical stopping but a growth stoppage. As long as you're still moving forward in growth many of your problems will disappear. Additionally, don't be surprised if some new problems and issues crop up as you go along. There is nothing that says things will always go smoothly. Unfortunately that is something that goes with the territory. Change and issues that go along with that. We can't always affect things happening to us but what we can always affect is our reaction to that.

CHAPTER TWELVE

IF IT AIN'T WROTE DOWN,
IT NEVER HAPPENED

This is a curious statement and it's certainly an awful use of the English language but I hope I got your attention. While this statement applies to everyone in every sphere of life, it is especially significant for Christians as we miss much of what is available for us by simply forgetting. You know, much of our Christian heritage comes down to us simply because somebody had the foresight to write it down. That may be one of the significant contributions of the Jewish people to the world, this very notion that they wrote it down. While other religions have also done this, no one has done it to the extent that the Jews did. As a result they developed a sense of identity through their religious history which is there for all to see. And that directly translated over to the development of Christianity. As we all know, the early church was started by Jews who identified and accepted the teachings of our Lord. They provided good training for the generations that followed.

One night recently, as I lay in bed, this great thought came me; a tremendous concept that directly related to this book. As I lay there the ideas just kept rolling across my mind. At that time there was no doubt that it was the Holy Spirit directing my thoughts, providing clarity, wanting to give me some direction. As I lay there with all those ideas and concepts flying across my mind, I reminded myself that I should get up and write some of those ideas down so that I wouldn't forget them by morning. After some due deliberation with myself I lost the argument. It seems that my ego, now that I'm writing this book, won't allow me to believe that I could forget something so important. Not! When I woke up the next morning, I remembered only one thing and that was that I needed to remember something important. It's been several weeks now and I still can't remember so I decided to move on. After some reflection on this matter it has occurred to me that I have made my life a pattern of this kind of attitude. Great ideas passing overhead and me superficially responding only to let them slip away into the darkness of my thoughts, probably never to return. And they were such great ideas too! Who knows what opportunities I may have missed over the years because of my inattentiveness to the leadership of the Holy Spirit as my spirit tunes into him. Has that kind of memory lapse ever occurred to you? You know, we need to be sensitive to the leadership of the Spirit, especially at night when we're winding down. When we relax is when we're receptive. Think about it,

One of the great strengths of Judaism, the basis for all monotheistic religions, is that the Jews wrote everything down, be it the direct words of God to the thoughts and actions of the people, to a steamy book that rates right up there with the best of them. Quite frankly, the Jews continued that tradition of writing everything down through the Diaspora until today. If you ask a Jew what the contributions of Judaism to civilization is, one of the frequent answers you would get is ideas. The notion of keeping a written memory of something is so that we never forget. Many people get tired of hearing, seeing and reading about the holocaust. It's time to put that behind us they say. It's time to bury the past and move on. The Jews on the other hand, as Elie Wiesel the Nobel Laureate postulates, believe that the record needs to be clear, vibrant and with us, so that future generations do not forget the atrocities committed by man against man. Ethnic memory is of utmost importance to Jewish culture. It's how they function. It's how they have functioned and will function into the future. And thank God for that because it is in their faithfulness to that aspect of their faith that we have our Scriptures today.

The history of the Jews ought to be enough to remind me of this concept especially when I, as a believer, reflect back on God's leading, revealing and great love for us. While this has not entirely registered in my brain there are other issues that have contributed to my dealing with this concept. While I was in Seminary studying for the ministry, I was introduced to the Concept of 2959. Some of you may be familiar with that program. It is essentially a program, designed by Peter Lord, whereby you spend one half hour daily in prayer and bible study. And while doing so you write down the thoughts the Spirit impresses on you in both your reading of the Scriptures as well as your prayers. It sounds like a piece of cake, doesn't it? Only one half hour per day. It doesn't sound like, much yet most Christians don't give our Lord that much time. Nonetheless, there is more to this than just putting you on a guilt trip, which is not my intention; in fact I apologize if I did that because I think there is too much of that in the Church today.

At any rate, the point I'm trying to make is that the writing down of thoughts and impressions as you go through personal bible study and prayer are revolutionary tools for growth. Now maybe I didn't understand the concept in the early years, or maybe it wasn't explained right or maybe I was just too lazy to implement the concept in my own life. Nonetheless, I finally picked up the 2959 after several years on the shelf; dusted it off and read my scattered entries from several years earlier. It was amazing. There was my spiritual life, right in front of me and it was so fragmented and incomplete. I was crushed by the shallowness of my relationship to God. Yet on the other hand it became evident to me that if it ain't wrote down, it's like it never happened. The memories fade of what hasn't been written down until soon it is not even a part of your life anymore. But yet what was written becomes part of your Christian identity, your relationship to God. It's more than a diary it is a permanent record of your growth experience in the Lord.

Just think about why you take pictures of your children, beginning from when they were babies. You do it partly so you have a memory of what they were like at various stages of their lives. It's the same with personal bible study and prayer. How can you ever know if you've grown or changed as a person or as a child of God if you have no record? He knows but you don't. Soon your memory of God's grace, of his great love, of his blessings, of his exhortations, fade as does the day into twilight and then darkness; soon the image fades from our mind, when we no longer see ourselves in the mirror of our individual ethnic memory as a son or daughter of God and we go back to the monotony of life which oftentimes carries with it very little excitement, no vividness, no anticipation of the future. Why? Because our lives are like they never happened. Where is the record? No record, as the sands of time pass us by, it's like it never happened. Remember, we *do life*. We are not passive, we are *doers* and writing it down is a part of *doing*. In this sense, *doing* is not physically taking on more tasks but rather be an active, participant in everything that life throws at you. In many ways, *doing as I use the word* can be more appropriately be used as *being* yet I find that most people don't understand the concept of being so *doing*, as it connotes the idea of activity is a better descriptor even though it sometimes becomes obfuscated by those who still believe that works is superior to faith.

As Christians we fall into several traps that rob us of the joy of our salvation. One of those traps is that we abdicate our right to think by letting others do it for us, be it the pastor, our spouse, our boss, the television, whatever. The other trap is that when we do have a thought that brings the excitement back into our life, a thought that actually expresses a kernel of truth revealed by the father we promptly forget about it. Is it any wonder that we are a generation of shiftless people, with no roots so that we can be swayed in our thoughts, opinions and relationships? I see people writing down notes in church all the time, trying to get down every word that the pastor expounds upon so that he can be quoted in every subsequent conversation - to validate some dogmatic point that they're trying to make. They, more often than not have no clue what the pastor said, or what it means, and because it's the pastor's thoughts and words, not their own, the words, thoughts and concepts become faint after the passage of time. It is in my judgment, much more effective, to make a note of the highlights of the facts, to ponder over them immediately after the sermon, incorporate them into your thinking pattern and then file the whole treatise for future reference. Think about what's been said, analyze it, confirm it through additional research and then commit it to paper.

When we hear that we have become a generation of sponges it's not because we don't have the capacity to be more, it's because we don't take or make the time to be more. Notice, that in this case I didn't say do more, I said be more. We already do more than we physically can (at least in the sense of *works)*. We're tired, exhausted; so while we can't do more we do have the capacity to be more. All it takes is the realization that we must be more effective in using the time that we have allotted to us. We must be wiser. So when you pray and read your bible, do so with pen and paper. You say, I'm already doing that so your telling me nothing new! How about, during the day when the Holy Spirit impresses a thought in your heart and on your mind? You say to yourself, that's pretty neat, but I'm busy now, I'll get back to that later. How many times have you gotten back to that later? You promptly go back to your work, go about your business, never to return to that thought. If you really are that busy, scribble that thought on a piece of paper so that you can return to it later and when you get home, pull that crumpled piece of paper out of your pocket and God, in his wisdom and through his grace can begin spinning a new web in your life.

I keep hearing the complaint that I'm not organized enough to write something down. Frankly, this concept has nothing to do with organization. It has everything to do with being wise and a good steward of what God has given you. What do we all have in common? Rich or poor? Wise or ignorant? Popular or unpopular? In good health or in poor health? You say you're just a nothing, an ordinary average person. Do you know that you have a gift that is equal to that which even the most powerful of men have in the same proportion? Yes, it's true. TIME. No more, no less. Each man has the same amount of time allotted to him each day. What you do with it is what separates the average from the great, from the haves and the have nots, from the fulfilled and the unfulfilled.

Now, I'm not advocating that you can or should immediately aspire to be great, rich or powerful. That's a subject for another time and place. What I am advocating is that you, only you, are responsible for giving your life meaning and purpose. And you can do it quite simply by living a little smarter, not a little harder.

I've always admired people who keep daily journals. I've admired the consistency with they've lived their lives. I'm not saying that they're better, just more consistent. My son is one of those individuals who has gotten himself into one of those positive rhythms. What I admire in those kind of individuals is what they pass on to future generations as well as giving themselves an ongoing gauge for the here and now. Reading the journals of the great and not-so-great, long after they have departed this world is really amazing. It lets you into their being, into their hearts. Now, you don't know what your life will bring, what impact it will have on future generations. All you know is that you struggle each day and seem to gradually lose ground.

While you believe that you're going to heaven, you wish you could go now. The burden is so heavy and to top it off you see no value in your existence. There is no contribution for you to make. NOT!

Write it down! Even that one, negative, desperate thought! It's you! It's where you're at! And someday, when you see that slip of paper tucked away in a desk drawer, a book, wherever, it will either remind you of how God delivered you or will bring to your conscious self something to which you still need to bring some closure. And even when you're gone, to be with the Lord, maybe someday your grandchild, in a moment of despair, will be thumbing through that book and see that note, that thought. And he or she will make a mental note that it's ok to be alone, to be frightened, to be scared. It happened to grandpa too. Any legacy we leave is found in the most simple of places - the heart. That's what we leave behind. And remember, just because you have a thought that is not always upbeat it's not a sin to make a note of it. It's not Satan driving a wedge in your spiritual life. It's you. And you can demonstrate your faith by noting, like David, those moments of despair as well as those moments of deliverance.

So as you reflect on these things remember that writing it down makes it real - for you NOW as well as for future generations. Your words, your thoughts are you. That's what Judaism, as the forerunner of Christianity gave us in addition to Jesus; they gave us an ethnic memory, thoughts of the heart that tie us to God forever. Don't be lax in this one area that truly gives you an identity that makes you the unique individual that you are in God's eyes as well as in the eyes of those with whom you come into contact. You don't have to be a great theoretician like Einstein, or a thinker like Plato. You don't even have to be a popular writer like Tom Clancy, Danielle Steele or John Grisham. Just be you! You with infinite worth and value beyond measure. I have spent a lifetime around older people and as these people grow older many of them lose their capacity to remember; be it dementia or Alzheimers, or whatever. I have noted that the stories that are pent up inside these individuals could be a valuable lesson for all of us. Something is always struggling to get out and when the memory becomes dim it's lost, perhaps forever. Write it down. Your thoughts, your story, your pilgrimage; it could have a great impact on someone besides yourself. If not today, then perhaps tomorrow.

But, you say, God hasn't chosen me to have an impact on anybody or anything. I'm just a laborer, a homemaker, whatever; working my way through life one day at a time. God may not have chosen you for greatness today but how do you know about tomorrow? Many great artists, writers, leaders are not remembered during their lifetimes; many times it is the generations that follow who remember them by their deeds, works and words and elevate them to the forefront through their memories. Read that great roll call of the heroes of the faith in Hebrews 11. Many of those individuals you certainly never heard of. So if God gives you a thought right now, why can't it be for something that counts. Don't say I'll finish reading this chapter and then write it down. Do it now! My words will still be there, but your thoughts may not. Remember, if it ain't wrote down, it didn't happen.

CHAPTER THIRTEEN

ALL ABOUT MIRRORS

Scripture tells us that we are created in the *image of God*. (Genesis 1:27). But what does this really mean? Many people have believed, over the centuries, that this is an indication of our physical attributes subsequently explaining our human conception of God, i.e., the fatherly figure in flowing robes with the long white beard, sitting on a throne somewhere high in the spiritual realms. While that may, for some of us, be a portrayal of our relationship to God it is a superficial one at best. Others have tended to reflect on this concept of God in a more cerebral manner. We are, after all, the only creation that has the (alleged) ability to reason, be it for good or for bad. Even though we have many of the basic instincts of animals, such as the need for food, shelter, clothing, sex, survival, etc. it is our alleged ability to use our minds that separates us from the rest of the animal kingdom. Others tend to see humans in a more spiritual sense. It is attributes such as love, hope, charity, justice, mercy, power, etc. that fix us on a plane above the rest of creation. Additionally, we have further concepts about this notion. Because we don't really have a good conceptual handle of God in a realistic sense of the word we have a tendency to relegate him solely to the spiritual world and mystify the general concept of who he really is. And because we can't relate to our idea, or anyone else's for that matter, we have a tendency to compartmentalize our lives in relation to our understanding of God and the role that he plays in our lives. And, because our understanding is so limited we further relegate some things to God and other things to Satan. For example, if we can't explain an occurrence, or non occurrence, we either say God allowed it to happen or that Satan is interfering. Our sense of individual responsibility has diminished, or at best has become confused and entangled in the quagmire of our twentieth century existence.

It is true, however, that the world is subject to a number of forces. To be sure God plays a direct role in the affairs of men. He still moves stones, each and every day. Satan, on the other hand, also plays a direct role in the lives of men. As the prince of darkness, he lays bare to men all that is superficially good but inherently bad. But, this section is not about God or Satan, it is about us. How do we fit into this drama? What roles do we have and how do we affect those roles?

In my mind these questions have a lot to do with mirrors. Now, what on earth do mirrors have with our relationship to God, ourselves and our ultimate reality. And how can we use this concept to develop a more cohesive and well-balanced lifestyle which is not only a joy to live but also a life that bring pleasure to God.

First, what is a mirror? We are used to seeing mirrors as a form of polished glass with some kind of silver coating on the back which provides a clear reflection. Other highly polished surfaces also provide reflections, albeit not as precisely or consistently as our mirrors of glass. It is the mirror of glass that I believe has a story to tell us and provides a framework for accessing the almighty.

In its initial phases a mirror gives us a reflection of our physical selves. The person we see is a reflection of the individual created in God's image. The wonderful thing about this image is that it represents the outer covering of who we are. Additionally, every person reflected in this mirror appears differently, at least outwardly, from other reflections. It is this initial reflection that grabs our attention. We spend time in front of the mirror. Men use it for shaving, combing their hair, whatever; women use mirrors to put on their make up, and so on. Our self perceived image is so important to us that we oftentimes rest and linger at the point of reflection.

Unfortunately mirrors can break or fade. Of course, when they break, there is no more reflection and when they fade they become blurred at the edges until at some point they no longer provide the image that we have become accustomed in seeing. In both of these instances we usually immediately go out and replace the mirror because we have this innate need to always see as clear an image as possible.

It is, however, in the fading of the mirror that we can find our real selves. In 1 Corinthians 13:12 Paul talks about mirrors being a *poor reflection* and they really are. The crisp, new mirror provides a physical reflection of the shell of the person who really is more than flesh and bone. It is a reflection of a *mensch*, a person, an individual, human being. As we grow older Paul goes on to say, that as we develop and mature, childish things become passé and adult things move to the forefront. The image is no longer as important. He's not speaking of physical attributes here, he's speaking of concepts that we never have really learned to practice. Those things such as faith, hope and love which at the core of our being are so much more important than what we look like.

And as our mirror fades physically, so should it fade spiritually. Don't replace the mirror when it fades. Keep the old mirror to see God. If you practice getting to know him, getting to understand him, letting him work in your life, the fading mirror takes on new meaning. Your concern for the look of the crisp physical body, this earthly tent, gives way to a reflection that begins to intertwine with God. The concepts of faith, hope and love take on different meanings, they take on real meanings; as the mirror fades you place less emphasis on yourself and more on what is behind yourself. All of a sudden it is not so important of what you look like but who you are.

Most people would agree that it really is a superficial world in which we live. We give lip service to not liking what we see, the violence, the worship of self, the greed, but we carry on anyway. I don't advocate breaking the mirror; God can break the mirror anytime he wants. And when he does then you'll be apprehended by a force that goes beyond anything that you've ever imagined. Because, you see, when the mirror is broken we find that the reflection was really God. He's the silver backing behind the glass. He not only is the basis that causes the reflection but also the glue that holds the mirror together.

For most of us, however, the mirror doesn't get broken. It only fades. And as we grow in grace we find that the image really is the creation of God. He is the silver paint back of the glass. And as it is handled, over the course of time, the silver wears off. Torn, little holes appear. Finally, after a period of time we can see right through the glass again. There is no more reflection. At that point we need to recognize our wholeness. A clearer image of God should have gradually supplanted the silver backing of the mirror. So if you're seeking his will and wanting to become conformed in his image, take the time to rub the back of the mirror. Get steeped, immersed in faith, hope and love. Begin to see the world through the eyes of him who created you in his likeness. Rub the faith, rub the hope, rub the love that knows no end. Be feverish in your stance. Don't give up. Faith doesn't give up. Don't let Satan rob you of your hope; after all he has no hope. Above all rub, the love of Jesus onto your life.

How do you do this? How can you make the image become less of you and more of God? It's really quite simple, just do it. Spend more time in prayer than looking in the mirror. Let him speak to you through his word. But, you say, I don't have time. I have to earn a living. I have a family to support and to take care of. I need sleep. I need to eat. I need time to myself, to recharge my physical batteries. There you go again - it's the mirror - you see nothing but yourself and all those personal issues so clearly. The issues of daily living have personified your image of you!

However, don't you believe that God can help you deal with those issues? If you really believe that then you've got to rub the back of the mirror. You need to get more of that silver backing off. Get up early or stay up late. God wants you to rub the mirror, not just look at it. When you look you see only your personal needs and problems. As you rub prayer, as you rub faith, as you rub hope, as you rub obedience, as you rub listening is when you will see the self image becoming more and more blurry. And as your self image becomes more blurry you will see God becoming more and more clear. He talks to you. He walks with you. You see him acting on your behalf. Getting rid of the self image, that of hopelessness, unloveliness, helplessness and fear works only as effectively as you are dedicated and willing. Notice, I didn't say you had to be effective, only dedicated and willing.

As you look in the mirror you see the one person who can effectively remove all the burdens and issues of the day. You are the only person who can move you to other heights and worlds. YOU, and yet NOT YOU! CHRIST within you! The one in the mirror, not behind it. He may ask you to break the mirror or he may tell you to just keep rubbing it. You won't know which until you start rubbing.

They say that breaking a mirror is bad luck; 7 years worth. I've found that God sometimes wants us to break the mirror. Sometimes he can't do anything with us until it's broken. That doesn't happen arbitrarily or in a vacuum, however, it generally happens when you are in the process of rubbing it, trying to see your image conform to him. Then at some point he may say it's time to break the mirror. He may ask you to leave a position, reject a lifestyle or a habit. It could be anything but it's oftentimes something that you are afraid of dealing with. It is at that point, when the mirror is broken, so that you are one with God, when faith takes over and articulates his miracle for your life, that your own self image is totally obliterated, then and only then will you see the real you.

I remember one time this happened to me. I was desperate. Nothing was working out. I had more month than I had income. I got up early each day and prayed and stayed in the Word. I kept rubbing. Nothing happened on the outside but in the inside I was changing. Finally, one day God told me to break the mirror. That I needed to leave where I was at, so that he could take me to where I needed to be. But he couldn't do it as long as I had the mirror in my hand. So I broke the mirror. I left where I was at. I moved forward, without a (physical) place to go but resting in the image and grace of God. Within 30 days my world had changed. I soon had more income than month. But more importantly I had a newly developed sense of self, of self worth, one that was bound up in God and not me.

Sadly though, after a while, I picked up a new mirror because the old mirror held too many memories for me, had too much of a grasp over my life. I had forgotten the lessons that God had taught me so quickly. I had forgotten that he was in the mirror, that I had actually touched Him, that he actually entered my world. So before I really knew what had happened, because I didn't stop to reflect I had put myself in the position that I had to start the process all over again.

CHAPTER FOURTEEN

AFTER 2000 YEARS, IS THIS ALL I GET?

A troubling question for many people is not always necessarily regarding Jesus and his message but is more specifically directed at the church. (Notice, that I use lowercase c not uppercase C) The question surrounding the value of institutions is certainly a modern phenomena that grows proportionately to the advancement of civilization. While becoming a distinctive 20th century problem, especially with the talk of a new world order, the issue of institutionalization does have its roots in history.

The institutionalization of the church really began with the advent of the Roman emperor Constantine who in the 4th Century A.D. declared Christianity the faith of the realm. While the process of institutionalizing the church had obviously been in the works prior to that point, it was this formalization of the state with the church gave impetus to the development of the institution of the church. And since that time it has certainly developed. I don't claim to an historian so I'll leave the detailed discussions regarding this subject to individuals more qualified than myself, but as a layman, I see here a tragic development in the practice of religion as we know it. We have, over the centuries, developed a tendency to put our trust in this institution and its people rather than in God. To some extent I suppose that I can understand that development. Just as it isn't guns that kill, but people the same principle applies to the church. It is isn't the church that errs but some individuals within the church who have gone overboard. Or is it? The same argument applies to our political system. The president may be a total bozo but we enshrine the institution of the presidency. So to that extent then, we have moved institutions to the forefront of our thinking. As long as we have a mechanism whereby we can drive out the money changers from the Temple then we are ok. After all, it's the institution that matters, not people.

If the church, as an institution is viewed as a bulwark, academically or otherwise, against the *gates of hell* as we note in Peter's confession and is legitimized accordingly we have really missed the boat. And I do say this reverently. Nowhere do I read in Scripture that Jesus was advocating the establishment of a new institution. What he was advocating was that institutions would become unnecessary as people allowed the Holy Spirit to move in their lives. After all, Jesus had quite enough of the institutions of the Scribes and Pharisees.

On the one hand we revere the institution, the church. Yet we see where many public polls show that a majority of people give lip service to God but the pews are empty on Sunday. That fact alone doesn't bother me. In fact, many of our churches should be empty. If what comes out of many of these churches is anything like what comes across the air waves or the medium of television, the resounding cacophony is such that I oftentimes really can't understand why anybody ever wants to enter a church. Have you ever listened, really listened, to several messages of preachers back to back? If you are any kind of student of the Word, and have any sensitivity towards the leadership of the Holy Spirit, I guarantee you that the contradictions coming out of the mouths of many of these preachers is amazing. Then again, maybe you do understand and that is why thousands of preachers leave or are asked to leave churches every year.

We have a cute saying in our society - *ministerially speaking* - which is really a religious euphemism for saying *stretching the truth*. This is where the point is exaggerated to such an extent that it no longer has any validity as a real point. Many people would call that deceit, lying. etc. My point here is not to knock the church as much as it is to lament about where we are. After 2000 years, we have a message, still as true as it ever was and as vibrant and as necessary, but it has become lost in a maze of institutionalization, operating under the guise of evangelism but really committed to the idea of building empires, both large and small. This may be one of those times that the duck theory really doesn't apply. Just because it looks like a duck, sounds like a duck, feels like a duck, doesn't necessarily make it a duck in this case.

If you belong to a large church (or just attend one) why don't you test this for yourself. Just try to see the pastor if you're an *ordinary* lay person in that church. If you're really fortunate, you will be subjected to a scrutinizing pastor's secretary who has learned her screening techniques from Attila the Hun. More than likely you will get passed on to some assistant pastor who is *better equipped* to handle or deal with your specific problem. Funny, but I don't recall Jesus saying to the blind man, *speak to my associate Peter, he can help you with your problem*. There is no question that the issue of power for pastors of large churches is pervasive. The message, the message of love and understanding sounds good but is hollow. That's what institutionalization does, makes *hollow* something that is inherently good. In one sense, the idea of institutionalization rings a positive chord. For instance, if a pastor leaves for another parish the whole thing doesn't collapse. After all, we now have an infrastructure that keeps things floating until we get a new pastor. The flip side of that coin, however, is that the infrastructure of the church has created its own power hierarchy and it is this hierarchy that then dictates to the people. This is how church dogma is formed and then propagated. Through the hierarchy! That is not what Jesus had in mind.

Small churches, on the other hand, suffer from a different syndrome. These wanna be pastors have (or attempt to have) the ability to articulate their position to a small cadre of loyal believers who, it oftentimes seems, have checked their brains at the door. These congregations really want to be sheep but for reasons different than in larger churches. In larger churches people oftentimes want to be lost in a crowd so it is convenient to be a follower as it requires so much less energy. In a small environment you really have to consciously give up some basic rights as a believer. In either case, however, you've given up your personal rights to the institution who now is going to tell you what to think and believe. And this holds true for all situations, be they totally to the right or totally to the left.

The thing that really distresses me about this whole notion of institutionalization is that after 2000 years I sometime feel that I have nothing to show for my faith. Large churches are centers for egomaniacal leaders and small churches are bastions for subgroup diversions, neither of which most times provide any real relief for a people who seek refuge from the onslaught of secular institutionalization and the general attacks of everyday living. Add to that the church/state issues of the U.S., where issues such as prayer in school get batted around, and it soon becomes apparent that present generations are left to their own devices regarding spiritual issues. And while Christianity is an individual-based religion, the support mechanisms such as training have become lost in a sea of self servingness. If you don't believe me check out what 5 media pastors send you, compare the material and then decide which one is correct. No wonder we have a zillion churches but no place of refuge. If we would get off issues and get on Jesus then we might have a chance. If one tenth of the energy *spent* on issue oriented theology would be spent on changing the heart then the issues that we so steadfastly pursue would be no issues at all. Is this all I get after 2000 years? Is this all Jesus has to show for his death and resurrection? Is this what Paul, Peter and the other apostles had in mind as they took the Message, the Good News, to the four ends of the earth? There's got to be a better way than the fragmentation that has occurred over the centuries. This was not what was in mind.

That's not to say that social issues are to be ignored for we certainly have plenty to do in our affluent society. What it does reflect, however, is that our energies are directed to fighting Satan on his terms, on his turf, using his tactics. And on that basis we have abrogated our rights to the *new heart* that God wants to give us. So we still wait for the opportunity to usher in a new world. All of the evangelism in the world will not usher in the Kingdom. In fact, unless we change our hearts we'll still be here another millennium.

CHAPTER FIFTEEN

LOSE YOUR COMMON SENSE

Benjamin Franklin once said that the outstanding quality of common sense was that it wasn't very common. And as I look around me I certainly to see the evidence of that statement. People do the stupidest and strangest things at times; I'm certainly no exception. I know that fire burns and I also know that the results of burns can last a lifetime. But I still oftentimes find myself playing with fire.

I had just graduated from high school and was looking forward to my freshman year in college. As a young seventeen year old I had dreams that I hadn't even defined yet. One Saturday night my mother and I arrived home from work when the phone was ringing as we were walking through the door. It was the police. My father hand been in a terrible accident, a fire. As we arrived at the scene a few minutes later, I remember seeing my father being helped into the ambulance, second and third degree burns to over 50% of his body, the stench of burning flesh and the horrific sight of partially burned skin hanging from his limbs still haunts me to this day. It took a long time for him to get out of the hospital and today, 30 years later he still bears the scars of that fire. And every time the weather turns cold, the thin new skin provided by skin grafts to his legs continuously break open, as a reminder of a careless act more than 30 years ago.

You would think that I would be more cautious around fire; after all, my world as I knew it almost came to a grinding halt back then. It certainly changed as my entry to college was delayed for almost a year as I had to help my mother in running the family business. Yet as I reflect back on the past 30 years I note that when it comes to fire I try to be very cautious. I try to be circumspect in the way I treat anything that could potentially be hot. Yet there have been occasions when I exercised poor judgment, even when it comes to fire and things hot. I remember the time I tried igniting a recalcitrant barbecue fire by *throwing* gasoline out of a gas can onto the smoldering charcoal embers. The theory was that I had to get the fire moving along more quickly, I was hungry. What happened next was most interesting as I not only lit the fire in the barbecue, I also got the fire line going to the gas can. In my desperation I flung the gas can as far away from me as possible. Guess where it landed. By my car! Whoops. Without belaboring the point any further all I can say is that common sense is required in every aspect of daily living. Yet even when we know better, we oftentimes do stupid things that can have far reaching and long lasting consequences. We say that we should engage *brain* first but that is oftentimes the last thing brought into the equation.

Most of the time the silly things we do create difficulties for us when we don't stop to think about the consequences about what we're about to do. Usually we just do it. So often we operate on the basis of being reactive rather than being proactive and sometimes the reasoning isn't even that sophisticated, it's just an impulse. Nonetheless, regardless of what process aids in the creation of the dilemma we all pay the price for our lack of judgment and common sense. Remember the time you didn't have a pot holder handy and you took the iron skillet off the stove with your bare hands? How long did your fingers ache after that experience? How long did it take before you did it again?

I think we all realize that we could stand to have better judgment at times. That we would consider each situation and what really is required to deal appropriately in that situation. We even go so far to make the exercising of sound judgment a major element in our child rearing techniques. Our whole life revolves around trying to use sound judgment in any and all situations. We really try to emphasize that issue in our lives and many of us get better at it as we get older. The difficulty, however, arises in the spiritual realm and in this world which most of us cannot see, feel, hear and touch we find ourselves literally and figuratively in the dark.

In our western society we have become control freaks. No more, no less. Everything with which we become involved needs to be somehow controlled. And if we are not in the controlling situation we at least try to somehow implement some kind of framework around the situation in order to isolate the particular situation from the areas in which we do have control. Consequently we tend to lead disjointed, dysfunctional and schizoid lives - some more than others. And out of this milieu comes God. The one who asks that we recognize and acknowledge that any power we have really comes from him, that in the ultimate scheme of things whether it is issues of cosmological importance or in the details of everyday life it is he, God, who is in control.

While most people generally give verbal assent to the existence of God, they relegate him to only the spiritual world from where they believe they can summon his presence and purpose only in times of dire circumstance. You know, the basic idea of conjuring up God because his presence is required. Even believers, who state their undying allegiance to the one who died for our sins and rose again, have difficulty in recognizing that God is active in the details of their everyday living. The average person reading this is going to at least mentally say hogwash to this notion as they do not believe, in their heart, that God plays that kind of role in their lives. And you know what, they would be right, at least to the extent that God doesn't force his way into your life but he still controls circumstances and events for his purpose. So, if you don't let him in, of course, he may not play a direct role. Nonetheless, this perception is only partially true due to several reasons.

We humans have difficulty in imagining that an all powerful creator God could be interested in the affairs of *Joe or Josephine average*. While we recognize his omnipotence, omnipresence and power in our heads, we do not give the same assent in our heart. As a result God becomes powerless to work in our lives and we need to understand that. It is not enough to offer up our prayers, from brain to God through lips; they really must come from the heart. It is imperative for the heart to be in total sync with the brain. So how do you do that?

The first thing that needs to be done is to put God back into the center of our lives; not just the Universe. You would think that the reverse would be true, that it would be easier to put God in an area of our lives that we understand and that ascribing to him all the powers of the universe would be more difficult. Nonetheless, it is an accepted notion that God is God of the Universe, it's just our lives that he cannot get into. In that sense, then, we can accomplish our goals if we concede that the notion of *space and time* are human connotations, not Gods. If we can *really* see that then we can more easily adapt to the notion of God's involvement in our daily lives. Let me try to illustrate without being an egghead like so many who try to address this issue. In Genesis 1:5 we read, where after the separation of the light from the darkness, that God called the light *day* and the darkness *night*. In our finite minds we have begun counting the changes from day to night to day night and so on. Each time the sun comes up there is a new *day*. Off to work again, etc. Either the day is too long or the day is too short, depending on how busy we are. If we're really busy then *time* slips by without us ever thinking of God.

Consider, however, our astronauts for a moment, who whip around the earth 10-20-30 times per our *normal* 24-hour day. Have they covered more *days* because they saw light to dark to light to dark . . . 10,20 30 times? Of course not. The fact that we are always moving in and out of the spheres of darkness is a constant aspect of how the universal clock was put together. For God, however, if we ascribe to him the normal attributes that men give God, then light and darkness have to be simultaneous, two sides of the same coin, so to speak. That is why Peter can write in II Peter 3:8 that . . . *with the Lord a day is like a thousand years and a thousand years like a day.* The point is that to the creator of the Universe everything, with the exception of humanity, is just there, in its place, according to the plan. Humans, however, created in the image of God, do stand apart from the rest of creation, alongside God if they so choose. Unfortunately we never really did understand that relationship nor do we still. We have removed ourselves from our rightful place. The question is how do we get back to where we started. How do we restore ourselves to our rightful place?

This is where the platitudes coming from your average preacher aren't going to work for you. You, and you alone, have been empowered to move forward in your Christian walk, in your relationship to the Almighty. It doesn't have to bottom out before you can start moving upwards, even though that's usually how it happens as we never seem to learn as we generally look beyond activities of daily living. It really is quite simple; giving assent to the notion that you're not in control (never have been, are not now, never will be) is all it takes. Understanding that God really is continuously at work in our world is essential. Believing that He can and does work in our lives is crucial. It is at that point that you can say *Yes, Lord!*

Where this whole concept breaks down is in the perceived notion of the *easiness of Christianity*. We are so hung up on life in the 4th dimension that we have the mental image that it has to be just as easy for us to accomplish what we want in this world. We must start thinking in completeness, in unified terms rather than dualistically. When we do that, then we can give up our human egos and really conform to God's image. That's where the difficulty in Christianity comes in, namely giving up the control of our destinies in this life. It seems like when we get our eternity covered that we move back into and through *the garden that we have here on earth.* In many ways the death and resurrection of Jesus is much like the original sin; we have now eaten, we know what's right and yet we still won't do it. The Old Testament was right when it talked about the *stiff necked* Jews. Unfortunately, the spiritual graft of gentiles into the Jewish root has produced another race of *stiff necked* people. A race of people who still maintain that they know it all.

Letting go and letting God certainly goes against the grain for most of us. It certainly seems stupid and ill advised. Yet that is what is required. And that is when we lost our common sense, when give even that back to God. It is at that point that we can cause mountains to be removed into the sea.

CHAPTER SIXTEEN

ACCOUNTABILITY

I have noticed over the years that the issue of accountability or lack of accountability has permeated our society. This is evident in all strata of society, whether it is the public sector, the world of business and enterprise, the church, the family or the individual.

In recent years, during the Savings and Loan debacle we saw evidence of this in a grand way as banking and business leaders took advantage of the deregulation in the industry during the early 1980's. By stretching the limits of sound judgment and good business sense, many of these upper echelon leaders, through an audacity and greed previously unheard of, almost brought about the ruin of the financial fabric of this country. The personal quest to drink and get drunk on financial success has had major repercussions on the way business is done in America.

I remember the early 80's when bankers would loan money for oil & gas exploration and drilling without so much as blinking an eye. Major six, seven and eight figure speculative loans were made to individuals and corporations without any collateral other than what might come out of the ground sometime in the future. The Penn Square Bank failure in Oklahoma almost ruined the Continental Bank of Chicago, Illinois, at that time one of America's leading financial institutions, all because of greed, the notion of striking it rich without any sense of having worked for it. The craze in the oil patch then spilled over to real estate as people thought a speculative investment in something more tangible was the way to go. As in all situations some ingenuous individuals always find a way to circumvent normal and rational business practices by appealing to the greed in all of us.

It appears as if the notion of striking it rich is a fiber that is woven into the basic fabric of most, if not all Americans. We saw this in the gold rush days of the late 1800's in California and we continue to see it today. Even though most people in our society recognize that working is an essential part of survival, more and more people look for an easier way out. As Christians we are admonished and, indeed instructed to live by the notion that *by the sweat of our brow we will eat our food.* (Genesis 3:19) Nonetheless, there is something inherent in our human natures that drives us to look for a quick fix. I know that while modern society lays much of the blame for this ethical laxity on television, In this instance, I would, however, postulate that television is more a symptom for than a cause for our ills.

Business and public leaders epitomize much of the corruptness that permeates our society. One oftentimes finds a split personality in these echelons of society; there is a public persona which is warm, gracious and caring and there is also a private persona which is greedy, pernicious and totally void of ethical values. In this strata, the common byline often appears to be that nothing is bad, corrupt or evil unless you get caught. Hence it would appear as if the ethics center more around covering one's trail as opposed to doing what is right. Now, this is not to say that everyone in business falls in this category but we certainly have been exposed to enough of this in recent years to make us wonder as to how pervasive the problem really is.

Unfortunately the great unwashed masses, the majority, which casts judgment on this group also operates on a similar split persona. Their attitude appears to be one of pointing a finger publicly while privately wishing for an opportunity of having a crack at going for the brass ring. The general climate is one that we are responsible only to our feelings, wants and desires. If we get what we want then everything is O.K. If we do something wrong in trying to succeed, then the only failure is that we got caught. Then when we get caught the failure is recast onto a system whose rules and regulations are wrong because they appear to be exclusionary. Nobody admits to faulty or jaundiced motives, only to the expressing of regret (that we didn't get away with something.) It is no wonder then that many of the religious institutions that we revere suffer from the same malady that this world conveys as acceptable behavior; a world where the measuring stick of success is tied to the possessions and wealth that an individual or group has.

Some people will stop right here and discount reading any further by indicating that they have renounced the patterns and habits of this world and they, therefore, are immune from the susceptibilities and temptations of the flesh. Unfortunately, the metaphysical world suffers from the same maladies and escape is not entirely possible. As a result, in a general sense, the extension of lifestyle principles is oftentimes no different in the church than out of it.

In corporate life everything is justified and rationalized to the notion that decisions are made for the maximum benefit of the shareholders and investors in the corporation. In the church a similar justification is noted as inuring to the benefit of God and his people. After all, who can argue with the notion that *God told me*. If a pastor is chastised for following this logic, even though it goes beyond the bounds of good sense and/or practicability then the individual pointing the finger is deemed to be suffering from spiritual weakness, from listening to the devil rather to God. In this way many pastors develop a power and control over people that is not only unhealthy but dangerous.

It was Lord Acton who stated that *power corrupts and absolute power corrupts absolutely*. Translated to modern life we apply this principle to politics and business but we are hesitant to do so in the church. However, of all places where this axiom can readily be seen is in the corridors of ecclesiastical organizations. The *business* of the church has demonstrated that it is oftentimes even less inclined to conduct its business fairly and ethically than is the world.

In the world the issue of responsibility and accountability is contingent upon and subject to the laws of the land whether they are static or fluid. Hence the game of evading and/or avoiding responsibility becomes the focus of everyday living. Life is just too tough sometimes to constantly play by the rules. In the church, however, the issue of responsibility and accountability to an unchanging, immutable God presents some interesting anomalies.

Have you considered, for example, the world views of various subgroups within the Christian community? Why is there such a great disparity between these groups? Is one group right and one wrong? Are all right? Are all wrong?

How do you know for sure? The answers to all of these questions lie in one simple truth, namely that individual believers have abrogated the responsibility of being free moral agents to men and women who purportedly have the inside track to God. Their revelation reigns supreme. If you challenge them, you are of the devil. After all, you are not the pastor, you weren't called and you're not the anointed electronic evangelist who has the answers to life's questions.

Martin Luther tried to deal with this question when he developed his construct of *justification by faith* in his exposition of Romans. Since this revolution in the church we have come full circle as we once again find ourselves trusting leaders to do our thinking, praying, believing for us. Is it any wonder that your belief system yields no fruit, that it is stunted in growth, leaving you feeling helpless in a world where God doesn't care for you; a world where it is only the pastor, who sees his dreams and visions come to fruition?

The challenge is to become secure in your faith, individually, personally. Study the scriptures prayerfully. Believe in the promises. Openly challenge those leaders when they are incorrect. Challenge does not have to be belligerent, remember that. Also remember that they really have no greater gift than you, at least to the extent that you also are standing in the Holy of Holies, right now. Chances are you may be missing out on your blessing only because you are trying to get in on the coat tails of someone else, rather than get your own blessing, based on your relationship with God. While it is true that you should honor those religious leaders chosen by God, remember to test the spirits. If they do indeed confess that Jesus is Lord then you do have a good opportunity to do the right thing. If not, then you best move on.

So how do you test the spirits, you say. It's really quite simple whether you consider your own thoughts or actions, or those of others, including your leaders. The process starts with you considering the thoughts or actions prior to speaking or doing something. What are the consequences of your thoughts or actions (or those of others? Do you pass the test of sound judgment, wisdom and prudence? And as you *prayerfully* consider these things ask the Holy Spirit to guide you, to direct you. And while in this spirit of prayerful meditation ask the inner spirit which directs you to confess the Lordship of Jesus. If yes, then you may continue. If no, you'd better jump off that ship, now. That's your responsibility, your accountability. You see, if the spirit confesses the Lordship of Jesus while you're contemplating issues of significance to you, it is difficult to have *you* on the throne if you're really seeking God directly. Both you and God can't be on the throne at the same time. It is issues like these that James was speaking about when he brought up the subject of the tongue. It isn't just slander or hatred that the tongue espouses, but also the simple things, such as a yes or a no; things that can truly change the directions of relationships, of a personal history. Flip Wilson, in his monologues using Geraldine, used to employ the line . . . *the devil made me do it.* While this sounds good, it likely is not true. It is you who has the power to say yes or no. It's always your choice. And while Satan may place the temptations before you he cannot make you choose against your will. Remember to engage brain before engaging mouth. Engage brain before picking up a pen. Engage brain before moving your feet forward. That's your responsibility as a believer. You answer for your yes or no, not for someone else, including Satan. Nobody twists your arm but you. Remember it's easy to lay blame when things go badly. Conversely, when things go well, nobody gives you accolades for supporting them.

In summary then, accountability and responsibility are not to be construed as negative words or concepts but rather within the framework of empowerment. The moment you respond you are a responsible moral agent, accountable to God for yourself. It is at that moment that you begin to obtain the power you need, require and want. Each *yes* moves you another step forward just as each *no* moves you another step back, that is of course, assuming that your *no* was supposed to be a *yes*. Practical Christianity is like a steam locomotive where each thrust of power and energy gets the engine moving just a little faster; a *no* when a *yes* is required retards forward motion. Thereafter additional energy is required to move forward again. As you can well imagine it is much easier to keep moving forward as stopping and starting slows your motion towards the goal and consumes so much more energy.

As you say *yes* to the leadership of God, through prayer, meditation and the leadership of the Holy Spirit keep in mind that it is better not to do anything and keep moving at the speed you're at than it is to say *no* (when it should be yes) thereby slowing down the train and then have to crank up the old engine again. If necessary, move in small but deliberate steps along the way. In this way, the likelihood of constantly restarting the engine is significantly reduced and your energy requirements will be less. Additionally, by operating in such a fashion it will be less likely that you will give up due to the frustrations brought on by getting tired in your Christian walk.

In the world of business I have noted several things. An organization that is ordered and well run, requires (at least outwardly) less energy to perform. A new organization operates on sheer adrenalin (the excitement of doing something new). On the other hand, an organization in turmoil, constantly shifting and retracing its steps, expends so much energy to survive that nothing ever seems to get done. This is a good analogy for the Christian walk.

Nothing in Christianity is really as simple as many people make it out to be. Oh sure, the basic concept of the *leap of faith* in the acceptance of Jesus is simple enough. However, the *walk* is one that requires a serious commitment, The cost of discipleship, as Dietrich Bonhofer wrote, is quite high. It requires YOU! If you are a new believer, the sheer adrenalin will move you forward. There are, however, two options available when you leave *new* behind and move on. If you are ordered and disciplined, placing your priorities in proper perspective, understanding the principles of individual responsibility and accountability as well as understand the energy required to grow then you will not only function as a well-oiled machine but it will be with greater enthusiasm and less frustration. This does not mean that there will not be issues and obstacles along the way but you will be much better prepared to deal with them. Consider the help you have to do this. You have the Holy Spirit, who can energize even the angels of heaven to assist you on your journey. On the other hand, if your life is tumultuous and without peace it is time to consider your position on the accountability/responsibility spectrum. Are you consistent with your *ayes* and *nays*? Are you even thinking about your *ayes* and *nays*? Have you pondered the difficulties of why your Christian walk is so difficult so that you constantly whine and moan to the Lord? Have you been expounding on the energy used to move nowhere fast? If so, you may want to get back to the basics by reexamining where you are on the time line and begin anew - slowing and deliberately but with purpose, remembering that you and only you are accountable.

CHAPTER SEVENTEEN

THINGS THAT WORK,
THINGS THAT DON'T

The most important thing that I've noticed in my Christian walk is that I am a person, a free, independent agent, wondrously created in the image of God, with my own dreams and desires. The first thing I need to remember (and it took me a long time to learn this lesson) is that nobody answers for me. Like young Samuel, it is my responsibility alone to say, *speak Lord, for your servant listens.* (I Samuel 3:10) There is nothing difficult about this concept; yet at the same time it is likely the most difficult thing that you will ever do, the reason being that we are always so busy opening our mouths that we do not take the time to listen.

As a young business executive, prior to going on to Seminary, I had the opportunity to provide sales instruction as part of my varied tasks. I taught a course called *Professional Selling Skills.* Now, most people don't entirely understand the concept of selling as they tend to assume that selling skills are merely manipulative tools so that a particular service or product can be crammed down somebody's throat. After all, the sales person needs the money. Perhaps we've all had too many bad experiences dealing with used car salesmen, vacuum cleaner salesmen, or whatever. But it's not always about money. Good salespeople are taught that the most important element in the program is to *be a good listener.* Oh, to be sure the variations that spin off of this are immense as people do all kinds of things, such as manipulating verbiage, etc. But the bottom line is, that a good salesperson *listens to what you, the prospect, expresses as important to you.* The logic behind this is that if we *hear* the other person, really *hear*, then one of several things will happen. Either we determine that the individual is really no prospect at all and that we're wasting our time proceeding any further and that we should proceed to the next person, or we find out what the person really needs and/or wants at which point we can try to fill that person's need.

The walk of the believer is similar to that of the salesman/client but with several variations. Sometimes we're selling and sometimes God is selling. And while we may have some difficulty with that notion it is nonetheless true. Sometimes we want something from God, so we begin to plead our case, make our pitch as it were. At other times God wants something from us, usually our attention, and that's when the Holy Spirit goes to work in us. When we have on our salesman's hat, we never shut up long enough to hear what God is trying to tell us. We're behaving more like children than grown sons and daughters. In fact, we talk so much, we're so busy engaging mouth rather than brain, that if we hit the mark occasionally it generally is more a function of accident rather design.

Listening, while it sounds easy, is a rather difficult concept to master. Nobody, I repeat nobody, comes by it easy. Even Samuel took several shots at it before he got it right, and this was a guy dedicated to ministry and service, somebody already in the loop so to speak. If a guy like that can miss what's happening just imagine what the average believer goes through. Throughout the course of an average week you are bombarded by challenges and responsibilities within the workplace, by issues of time spent in automobiles and airplanes, the specter of children bombarded by conflicting values between home, school and play, etc. Additionally, the modern world of communications (Radio, TV, etc.) tends to confound, confuse and obfuscate as opposed to enlighten. The noise factor in our lives is incredible! Is it any wonder then, that with all this and more, that we have no concept about what listening is all about. The bottom line is that we're drowning and I'm saying *listen.* Now you really are up to your neck in alligators and it really is difficult to remember that your original objective was to drain the swamp.

Listening is difficult but it must be mastered if we are to truly lead successful and happy lives. It must become the single most important element of your everyday walk if you expect to escape the frustration that you presently experience. In your relationship to God this concept is just as important as it is in your personal relationships. The developing of effective listening skills is the single most important skill you will ever learn and ever need, both for your growth as a person and as a child of God. Not only does listening work but it is the most liberating concept that you will ever know. It will open for you vistas and horizons that may otherwise never have made it to your dreamscape. You will never be the same again. It works!

Unfortunately listening is not a skill with which we are born. We usually come into this world screaming and screeching and it seems that is how we want to play it all of our life. After all, it worked early, so why switch. Listening, however, is an acquired skill, and as an acquired skill it develops primarily as a function of the will. Simply put, much like Faith, you decide if, when and how you're going to listen. It is at this point that most people become totally confused and overwhelmed. Just as faith is a function of the will, so is listening. So how does this tie together? Simply put, the *will* becomes the operative word as is expressed in so much of Christianity. There is no word so powerful as *will*. *Will* activates hope and faith and listening and power and love. *Will not* activates the dark side of life, especially doing or not doing those things that you know ought to be done under a certain set of circumstances. *Will* really is a function of the choices we make. In I Chronicles 28:9 David charges Solomon to acknowledge God and to serve him with a *willing* mind. The word *will* allows us to seek out God. In the activation of that seeking out, God reveals himself to us and that is a function of the *will*.

I know that the detractors will decry the idea of the will as being the activating source of our belief structure. I would argue in response that the only people denouncing this argument are those who want to control you, those religious leaders who superficially and cursorarily disseminate scripture, while pontificating on a call to righteousness and holiness. Righteousness and holiness are not emotional responses! People need to know what the call to holiness and righteousness mean, and they need to be given the tools to move along that trail. This notion will further be refuted by those dialectical and philosophical theologians who will argue that the notion of the will is of lesser importance than other more endearing and basic concepts such as faith, redemption and covenant. And while these concepts are important in that they attempt to explain essential elements of our religious experience they *do not* set it in motion.

My response to these antithetical pontificates is simply this; neither pastors, media evangelists or philosophers live in the *real* world. Their comprehension of the essential is shrouded by the immediate, the ecclesiastical or the ethereal. This is much of what Jesus reacted against by deliberately taking his message into the pubic marketplace rather than into the halls of religion. By reflecting on the concept of *will* I am not saying that you can simply say *I will* to have the faith of an Abraham, to move mountains, etc. What I am saying is that the *will* is the requisite to the development of the listening skills which become paramount in the Christian walk. Who knows, maybe God has something infinitely greater for you to accomplish than for you to move a mountain, even though that is a pretty *cool* thought. Maybe moving you to listen to him is an infinitely greater task and accomplishment. It works, if you say *yes* as Solomon did. When Solomon took over the reigns of government from his father David, several things occurred simultaneously. First, his elevation to King came about as his devotion to duty and responsibility. When one looks at Solomon and his brother Absalom, we note that two basic characteristics surface. Absalom was his own man, with ego being the driving force. It ultimately led to his ruin and untimely death. Solomon on the other hand, while surely also having some ego, appeared to recognize, even above his training and education, that he was lacking in something intangible, something beyond himself. And as God asked him for his one desire (I Kings 3:4ff) Solomon asked for discernment and wisdom and the power to be wise in his dealing with his people. This was brought on by Solomon's initiation of the process by first going to God in prayer and that was a function of the *will*. The recognition, that no matter how powerful, how successful you are, no matter what kind of blood line you have, that there is someone with infinite greater power and wisdom than you, is a primary precondition to this whole exercise.

Keep in mind that the will is not some mysterious spiritual voodoo that you practice. It is, rather, a function of deliberately deciding on the path to be followed. In Solomon's case it was a deliberate function of putting himself in direct communion with God so that *His perfect Will* for his (Solomon's) life could be accomplished. Having the mind of Solomon, and taking specific steps to begin the journey of doing God's will is, unfortunately, not the trail that most of us start down. Our *modus operandi* is usually to begin the journey and then make corrections when obstacles are encountered along the way at which time we try to impose our feelings onto God. Then, as crisis managers, we try to tell God, that it is His Will that we are seeking, so therefore it should be done what we ask. At that point we have already missed the two essential elements. We have muddied the aspects of our *will* as well as convoluted the concept of listening.

I know that in a perfect world we would, as a matter of will, take a direct approach in listening to God. But, as we all know, it is not a perfect world (or should I restate this as follows: it's a perfect world inhabited by imperfect, fallen people). So how do we go about correcting our situation? If our initial objective really was to drain the swamp how do we get back to our original position? Problem solving such as this is really quite simple if some of the basic rules that we've talked about to this point are understood and observed.

In many ways our world, despite the technological breakthroughs of the 20th century, is as uncomplicated as it ever was, despite technological advancement. It still is a world of cause and effect. We do (or say) something, and then wait to see the results. Sometimes the outcomes are good and sometimes not so good. Even intended results sometimes have a way of becoming negative as other factors ultimately come into the picture. These other, unforeseen factors can really destroy a situation so that what appeared to be a good thing ultimately ends in disaster.

I would guess that the big question becomes one of correcting past mistakes and then moving forward. The central issues here are as follows:

1. We don't want to admit our mistake and defeat.
2. We don't want to admit that we erred in our original premise(s). Nobody is going to make us admit that our starting point was wrong.
3. We seem to feel that if we say we're sorry (to ourselves and God) that the difficulty will somehow magically go away, and it never does.

The bottom line is that while God can, he most times doesn't indiscriminately interfere in the issues of men. He is not our personal trouble shooter, our on-call genie to help us out in our time of need although he has functioned in that capacity from time to time. This doesn't mean that he won't help in time of trouble but setting him up to function *only that way* generally sets us up for disappointment. While God won't necessarily reverse the consequences of events that we put into motion he will work with us on the issues that got us there. So he helps us with those issues that led to our difficulties; he works in our heart, he changes our thinking process so that despite the consequences of events that may have transpired long ago, God can and will heal the root problem, not the symptom. But even that will not occur until the issues of the *will* and *listening* are addressed. So the issue of whining and crying when things get out of hand really doesn't work. You may evoke some self-pity and some sympathy from others but not necessarily a miracle from God. What does work, however in this syndrome is a return to the basics.

I have noted two things in life that seem to be a precedent to setting the stage for accomplishing your goals and being content. First, be concerned about and be a totally active participant in those things that you have control over. With regards to those areas, where you seem powerless, there is no reason to fret, just a reason to move past that issue and move forward. It is at that point that you are in a position for God to intervene if he so deems, and it is at that point that you usually will hear from him. I refer to this as the *cradle* effect. This is the point at which you finally revert back to the beginning, back to the basics. The logic behind this concept is that self-reliance has given way to God-reliance and this can only be accomplished by resorting to the implementation of your *will* so that you can and will *hear* God. I use the word *cradle* not because you are to be a taker only (as a baby is) but because you have placed yourself completely in the hands of God. In reality the *cradle effect* is generally a brief period of time but the beginning of a continuous spiritual state of mind. Maybe that's what Jesus meant when he said *You must be born again*. I do not believe that he ever intended that we should stay in that condition because that would then take away the *free will* aspects of our creation. This really is only the beginning point of our walk as believers. This cradle effect can sometimes be viewed as kaleidoscopic chamber where each facet takes on a different and fascinating hue of life. In this chamber you are at once free yet prisoner, helpless yet all powerful, blind but yet omniscient.

And while you are in this chamber, seemingly allegedly out of control, you are more in charge of your life than at any other point. The *cradle effect* puts you in the position of being like a sponge while simultaneously having control over what you receive and how you apply it. There is no point at which you do not have the power to say *yes* or to say *no*. Additionally there is no point that you do not have the ability to close your ears. The important thing to remember about the *cradle effect* is that it is not an automatic *forever* place so while you are there it is essential that you maximize your time and use it wisely. The reason I say this is not a forever place is due to the fact that the fickle nature of humans coupled with the capriciousness of life most times affects all of us to the extent that we revert back to old, self sufficient natures. You see, life in general, just like our relationship with God is not a straight upward moving line, nor is it a series of peaks and valleys that somehow keep pointing upward in a general long term slope; life is rather more like a series of ups coupled with plateaus that have occasional valleys in them. And that's not the way God designed life, it's just the way we humans apparently want to live our lives.

Just because I say that anything is possible if you put your mind to it and listen, really listen, as to how God is leading and directing, does not mean that you can automatically sustain life in this manner indefinitely. You will find, during the process that you leave the cocoon, go back out into the real world, spreading your personal wings, trying to implement what God has taught you along the way (or what you think God has taught you). Sometimes it may seem as if God, like a mother bird, has actually pushed you out of the nest, so that you are forced to fly. So whether it's just you yearning to be free or whether you sense that God has pushed you out of the cocoon there is a reason for it. Besides being in the hands of God you also are in the world and that's where you live, that's where God has you function.

I remember an extremely dark period in the life of me and my family. My financial empire (such as it was) crumbled, in fact disintegrated over night, Much of this had to do with my own egotistical decisions over the years. After working through the issues of accountability and responsibility, those issues of cause and effect, I finally admitted defeat and recognized my need to move on. My family life had virtually been torn apart. The only thing left for us was our faith and even that was getting pretty thin. After all, how could a God of love, grace and mercy keep us in such a place of utter despair. It just didn't make any sense, especially to my wife and I, who had both given our lives to the Lord at young ages.

It was at that point that I recognized my need to go back to the beginning, so I started doing things that I had done before but had let become minimal aspects of my life; things like prayer, meditation, contemplation, scripture study, everything! But I now had to do these things at a time and place inconvenient to me but convenient for God; usually at 5:00 in the morning, which is a real problem for a night owl like me. You see, when you're in the cradle, you have no choice as to the extent of the required commitment. A baby doesn't know that 5:00 a.m. is the time that parents want to sleep, a baby only knows that it is hungry or needs some other kind of attention. And it is to that extent that you must be pliable for God to work in your life. When you're hungry, wake up, so that God can feed you.

I must say that the first weeks of my particular exercise were extremely difficult. My prayer life, seemingly endless, actually lasted only minutes. However, as I moved from spiritual milk to loftier things my time went from a few short minutes to hours and then I didn't want to stop. There was never a day that God didn't have a word for me, be it a word of instruction, rebuke or exhortation. During this period I was still faced with my challenges and issues and while external things were not changing I was. I knew that these issues weren't going away but I also was absolutely convinced and confident that something was going on that would ultimately move me past my present circumstances. Needless to say, after a number of months, God spoke to me clearly and directly. He gave me my marching orders; it was time to move on and I did.

The point here was that the *cradle effect* while essential was also only semi-permanent. Listening to God and making your faith a matter of the will always takes time and effort. The reason I say this place is temporary is because the issues of life always take time also and when God gives you your marching orders he knows what energy it's going to take, the effort you're going to have to expend. So when you find yourself out of the cradle, implementing what God has given you do not be discouraged or frustrated that you can't get back to where you were. Furthermore, don't even try. Once you've left the cradle there is something else required and that is for you to determine in concert with God. It is a big mistake to assume that you're going to stay in the cradle, that you can stay where you're at. Yet we all automatically gravitate towards that line of thinking and then wonder why there are no answers. God did it three years ago, when I got up at 5:00 a.m., why won't he respond now? Look forward, move forward. Remember, getting up at 5:00 a.m. to pray to pray (or whatever) was when you were in the cradle. Maybe today he wants you to stay up late, or take time during the day, whatever. Just be sensitive to his leading, remembering that making your faith a matter of the will is a key initial ingredient to moving forward. This doesn't mean that we are to become robots or automatons, it simply means that we are sensitive to essentials of relationship communication.

There is an element that needs to be elaborated here and that is to make your faith your own. If you wish to be the driver of the car, with God at your side you must adopt a lifestyle and attitude that is uniquely yours. Your dreams, your visions, your blessings! You cannot live your spiritual life as an extension of what others believe and/or put into your head, whether it is your pastor or other believers. While it is important to listen to what others say, it is more important to spiritually and cognitively determine if the voices that are speaking to you are from God or if they are just speaking. If it is God speaking, listen, and try to apprehend what he's saying. Test the spirits and meditate on the word. If you determine that it isn't God speaking then move past the word, it's obviously not something to be dwelled on, no matter how good it may sound. Above all things, and in all things, let the Holy Spirit be your teacher, both in your spirit and through scripture. That is not to say that the word of others cannot be used as confirmation to what you have absorbed or cannot be used to move you from a present path that you're on. At all times test the spirits to determine if the word of others really is from the Lord. Remember, you're not a perfect being here, hopefully just an obedient one. There will be times that you're correct in your understanding just as there will be many times that you are completely wrong. Being wrong is no sin, it's just being wrong, if your deliberation put you on a wrong trail. The main thing to keep in mind is that, like Solomon, you have a willing heart that is teachable. You'll never always be right in your decisions. It's no sin to admit that you made a mistake, but it is a sin to develop a sense of arrogant pride that would admit nothing, ever. God told me! Could be true, could be hogwash? Develop your own dream, in conjunction with the leading of God. Your dreams can and will come true if they're from God. That is what leads to complete fulfillment. Adopting the dreams of others leads to nowhere and leads to living life in a vacuum with hollow dreams which are without fulfillment and incomplete. It doesn't work if it's not yours. It doesn't work if you don't decide to listen first.

Above all, remember one thing - be patient. You cannot undo a life of sin and unbelief, overnight, with one prayer. You cannot become a spirit filled, obedient believer just by saying the words, one time. It doesn't work that way. Like the development and growth of a child in a mother's womb, so is your life as a believer. Some things virtually develop immediately without asking for them, while other things have to gestate, develop and gradually grow before you can see the final product. The only way you can know where you are on this spectrum is to listen, listen, listen. You will know when to move forward and at that point all of the forces of darkness, of indecision, of fear will not be able to restrain you.

CHAPTER EIGHTEEN

IN BUSINESS WITH . . .

In our 20th century world we read and hear much about a social restructuring of our society, with homogenous groups banding together for a common purpose. Almost like large support groups. And some of this thinking has rubbed off on the Christian community at-large. Support your brother car repairman, support your sister insurance agent, etc. While a good concept in theory, indiscriminate applications of this thinking can be disastrous. A pet peeve of mine, crystallizing over the years, is the issue of doing business with and being in business with Christians. Like so many others, I have been burned by having had business relationships of some kind with so called believers. In fact when I look at what some of these alleged Christian business leaders do, and how they do it, apparently without regard for any kind of business ethic I am baffled and baffled. Furthermore, I can't believe that I never saw past the veneer to begin with. On the other hand I am not surprised! As early as the first church, even during apostolic times, we got a sense that Christian values expounded in the real world were not always morally upright. In the earliest churches life was not always a spiritual event; in fact, the pagan Roman population was appalled at the lifestyle of Christians as they lived morally debauched lives. That is our early history, I'm afraid, and we have to live with it. Even though some things have changed 2000 years later, many of those elements still remain. It seems that there has been and oftentimes still is an inherent tendency for Christians to think that they are above living life in harmony with the world in which they live. Even Jesus said, render unto Caesar what is Caesar's, and unto God what is God's. And while this can be construed to imply a definite line as living apart from society the argument simply cannot be justified that Christian values are always above the law.

There is nothing that says we can go out and kill, just because we believe a moral law of God is broken, such as killing abortion practicing doctors. Who elected us as judge, jury and executioner? At the same time, nowhere do I read in Scripture, that we are given the right to do slovenly work just be because we're Christians. If anything, our works ought to be exemplary, above reproach, so that the world will wonder what it is we have that they do not. Unfortunately, much of our work and business practices reflect anything but. Neither is it written anywhere that the end justifies the means, even if it's just the nonbeliever who's getting the shaft. Even when I try to disregard my own personal experiences, which generally have had an unhappy ending, probably because they have been tainted by past history, I find that other similar horror stories keep surfacing that bring me back to this issue. I guess the old adage of where there's smoke there's fire cannot be totally ignored.

The first issue that needs to be addressed is that of Christian institutions, including not-for-profit corporations, churches, evangelistic associations, etc. It has gotten to the point that whenever someone says trust me, send your money to me, without strings attached, of course, so that I can do the work of the Lord the first and only thing I can say to you is, turn and run like the blazes. Many ministry organizations, of all types, have tended to be run by autocratic rulers without the same kind of visible direction reserved for most public/private organizations. The worst thing that an individual can do is financially support a ministry whose only response is a quarterly newsletter. Have you ever considered the number of groups and organizations that line up to solicit your hard earned dollars? It's utterly amazing. They all want my support, prayer, financial and otherwise, but none really want any input from me. All they want is my financial support without any sense of reciprocal responsibility or accountability.

The local church also has some difficulties in this area. While a number of church groups practice sound fiscal policy, many do not. Those that do not are inspired by autocratic rulers who do not wish to be accountable to anyone and they use God as a final authority when it is obvious that not even God has a say in the matter. I can see God, right now, blanching at the sight of those egotists who hide behind His skirts to implement their ideas and programs, NOT God's! Last I heard, most preachers were called to preach; if they are called to be the chief executive officers of corporations they should have gone to business school rather than into ministry. Last time I checked, and certainly when I went to Seminary, there were no courses offered into the running of corporations disguised as ministries.

Now, I don't mean to say that all ministries fall into this category because there certainly are many who do a fine job, who pursue their mission and still maintain a certain decorum with regards to accountability and responsibility. On the other hand, there are far too many who totally disregard the lay membership of the organization, believing that either hype or guilt are the order of the day. As a result too many fine believers, with good hearts and exceptional minds, are turned off organized Christianity and move on. That really is too bad because we lose many potential leaders who could really be of great assistance to the cause as Christianity moves into the next millennium. And while the losing of these good people could be catastrophic for the church, it is those who remain that present a bigger problem. All too often, remaining behind in the fold are those fringe elements who are subject to the whims of self serving leaders, who themselves know only to cajole and incite and whose real understanding of the world in which we live is clouded by the very superficial attitudes that the majority is reacting to and attempting to escape from.

Additionally, we have those quasi religious corporations who capitalize on the weakness of good-hearted believers by hocking all kinds of services and products designed for the modern Christian believer. This is becoming very similar to the concept of *relic worship*, evidenced in the middle ages, when it was fashionable to want something that tied the faith back to the times of Jesus. These entrepreneurs then market their products or services using a slick Madison Avenue approach, combined with an aggressive twist on the Gospel. The bottom line is that these organizations care not one iota about the message but place all the value on the bottom line - their bottom line. Now, I do understand that a business needs to make a profit; otherwise it won't be a business very much longer and that might in fact eliminate a product or service from the market that really is beneficial and useful.

However, my question is this; where do we draw the line? Is it appropriate to use fear and other strong armed tactics just so that a profit can be made? I think of a national precious metals dealer who uses every known tactic of the world, and the church, to get people to buy his product. If he can't shame you to buy gold, silver or rare coins based on some obscure scriptural passage used out of context, then he'll try to scare you to do so based on an imminent eschatological end-of-the-world scenario. And if he can't do that he will tie this scenario to the ultra right wing politics which reads good but does nothing different than other extremist group. To top things off, this individual has absolutely no qualms about his marketing approach to those unsuspecting believers who listen to Christian radio or watch Christian TV. As long as a good profit can be made, so that he then can give big-time to the church, to show off God's blessings, then it is true that the end justifies the means. The fact that obscene markups are used on every product has no effect on this man. After all, using good business judgment, being fiscally sound yourself, is not the question. Just support me.

This really is a strange world, where even the church is being attacked by charlatans cloaked as fine believers, as upstanding pillars in the community of faith. And when these individuals and organizations come under public scrutiny they cry foul, and hide behind the curtains of the church, rallying support from a group of unsuspecting believers who could think for themselves, but refuse to do so, because the church supports the enterprise in question. I think of this national precious metals dealer who in the past 7 years has pleaded no contest in one federal case, lost a major tax case in state court and is presently in court for gouging customers with unconscionable markups. Some people would call this fraud. In the tax case he lost, the general merits of the case were that he intentionally treated his people in a manner that deprived them of benefits that employees normally receive; things like social security, unemployment benefits, etc. This was not done to protect them, as he so eloquently stated, but as the government correctly discerned, this was done out of clear violation of the law as well as to further line his pockets. The distressing thing about this case was that the pastor of the church that this individual so openly supported with his largesse continued to retain him as a confidant. What does that say to you about the relationship between the church and business?

The bottom line is this. There are unscrupulous people in the world. Some are of the world and some are so-called believers who are in the world. *Be as innocent as doves, yet as shrewd as snakes* in all your dealings. While you cannot know the heart of everyone, you can know your own heart. And under the guidance of the Holy Spirit you can develop a discerning spirit. Remember, you have just as much access to the truth as the next guy. Rely on your gut instincts, test the spirits and move in concert with God. Don't blindly accept what a person says he or she is, let their works demonstrate their fidelity to the Word. Where there's smoke there is often fire, and not just a little grease fire, but often a fire that not only is raging out of control but one that will consume you and perhaps ultimately drive you from the fellowship of believers because you were burned. Remember, the heart of men, is deceitful above all things and while I do not say trust no one I am saying that you should be careful and circumspect and not blindly accept what is thrown your way. This applies to national organizations, churches, large companies and the next door plumber. *Beware of wolves in sheep clothing!*

My wife is very good at reading situations; much better than me. When I used to come to her and relay information about the stated Christian fidelity and ethics of business associates or business people she would always point out to me that what they said were words. Until recently I disregarded her insight and believed my own instincts only to be burned by the self serving nature of man, that when things get tough the initial reaction is to turn to whatever it takes to survive. And while survival is good, it does not replace an abiding faith in the one who died for us and is intimately involved in our affairs. Survival gives no one the right to take advantage of someone who has placed complete trust in you based on what you say you believe. Remember, when you publicly announce your stand, you are held to a greater accountability and while you may think nobody is paying attention there abounds a great public scrutiny for those who profess to believe. Just ask Jim Bakker, Jim Swaggert or the countless number of other public religious leaders who have fallen in recent years and the number keeps growing. Be careful, be circumspect, be smart. Know who you're going into business with! When you give your money you're automatically a business partner. It's tough to hide your involvement from God, and hence yourself, even if you can hide it from men.

CHAPTER NINETEEN

NO FEAR

There is a T-shirt that I see people wearing all the time. It generally revolves around the notion that fear is not something to be avoided but to be addressed head on. While I appreciate and understand this concept there is a fallacy in the logic behind it that really needs to be addressed. Looking for issues that we can tackle are different than being prepared to deal with issues that come against us. Unfortunately, in our world we have developed a panic and anxiety mode that threatens to either drive us into utter seclusion or force us to aggressively draw a line in the sand over which no one can cross. While these two approaches are certainly obvious options, there is a third approach which I perceive as being even more pervasive and ultimately more dangerous and that is the notion of reacting to a world that stifles us by going out and looking for those things of which we are totally frightened and aggressively doing them to remove that particular phobia from our psyche.

The difficulty that I have with this is that people are having a tendency to react to fear as opposed to thinking through the consequences of just attacking the fear. In addition to that many Christians misapply the exhortation of Paul to Timothy in II Timothy 1:77 where Paul says that *God has not given us a spirit of fear, but a spirit of power, or love and a sound mind.* While some of the older translations use the word *fear* many of the newer translations use the word *timidity* which is a more accurate translation. The misapplication occurs when Christians take this out of context and apply it everyday life where the context specifically refers to the area of ministry, of preaching the good news. And while using this verse in additional situations is not always inappropriate, it is inappropriate when we arbitrarily remove it from *the* realm of the spiritual and want to arbitrarily apply it to worldly areas. I say this because fear is oftentimes an appropriate condition to be in and we must bear that in mind. Proverbs 1:7 says that *the fear of the Lord is the beginning of wisdom.* Keep in mind that if we take God out of the equation of our everyday lives then his power that we covet so much really becomes an illusion and all we're doing is fooling ourselves. It is only when we, under the leadership of God's Holy Spirit, move forward, into the realm that he is leading us into, that we can effectively and without second thoughts appropriate the veracity of Paul's admonition to Timothy. So when you have an inkling to attack those areas of everyday life, without being in the context of God's leadership, be extremely careful as it can come back to haunt you.

Using this incantation arbitrarily can create some real difficulties for us. Buying a handgun out of *fear* so that we can protect ourselves and our possessions may not be the wisest thing to do, if we do so without specific instruction. If we just move in that direction, the consequences may at some point overwhelm us. This is especially true in this violent society in which we live. Another area that should be of concern is in that of personal relationships. If you have an issue with co-workers, bosses, etc. and your personality trait is one of being submissive and reticent then it is dangerous to misapply Paul's statement indiscriminately and without God's leadership because it too may land you in a situation where you may not want to be. Confrontation, based on a false premise may further aggravate a situation or even get you fired, is a mishandled use of the concept of *fear.* These kinds of situations are especially dangerous for young people, who have been raised by television and have seen dead people come alive again next week, or highly charged negative situations miraculously resolved. They have no conception of the notion of consequences and blindly move where they oftentimes shouldn't and then they become victims of misapplied truths promulgated by teachings that are not only incoherent but cannot be substantiated by Scripture.

That's not to say that many aspects of Scripture cannot be moved into everyday living even if taken out of context and applied to everyday situations. But to do so indiscriminately, without prayerful consideration and without specific instruction from the Lord is foolhardy and can lead to self destruction. Satan likes nothing better than to have believers go off half-cocked because he knows that if those situations backfire, and they oftentimes will, that he then has a good hold on the individual. The worst thing that can happen, as far as Satan is concerned, is that nothing happens so the believer develops doubts in the efficacy and truth of God's word; the best thing that can happen, from Satan's perspective is that the whole thing will dramatically misfire, so that the situation gets worse or the consequences are catastrophic. In that case Satan now has extremely fertile ground on which to destroy the basis of a believer's faith. In either case Satan gets his way, an enigmatic and tentative believer.

If we let our children adopt a superficial attitude towards real life issues that can at best be counter productive and at worst be totally self destructive, then what does that say about our spiritual maturity? How can we blindly let our children forge ahead into areas that can result in permanent damage, if not to them physically but spiritually as well, Additionally, how can we delude ourselves into thinking that we are over comers in all things? Kenneth Copeland took some flack a few years ago by suggesting that we all have the innate ability to become Gods. By definition that notion implies that we have the power to sit in judgment and control over everything. The problem with that concept is not only that it is not scriptural; we are not going to become Gods but it is also self delusion in the worst sense of the word. We've not only misapplied Scripture but we set ourselves up for a mighty fall. In addition we then blame God for leading us astray and then, when we ask for help to escape the predicament that we ourselves so foolishly got ourselves into and not get it, then we have not only limited God but we have been spurious in our understanding of what he says. *No fear* sounds great, but is a greatly overrated concept that threatens to destroy our society, just as it already has woven itself into the very fabric of our being.

On the other hand, this notion of *no fear* has some tremendous upside for our daily walk. If we walk with the Lord and let him be our guide in everyday living and decisions pertaining thereto, then we really do have the potential to harness the creative and sustaining power of the Universe. If our approach to *no fear* is that we are afraid of what will happen if we are not obedient to the leadership and direction of God then we truly can, and indeed are mandated to have *no* fear. Then it is true, that *greater is he within us than he who is the world*. At that point we can truly remove mountains and cast them into the sea. Not only can we effect change in our lives by doing things that are generally not humanly possible but we can also effect change in a world that demonstrates self reliance as opposed to God reliance. The subtlety in the difference between what was discussed earlier and the power flowing through God's leadership is sometimes cloudy but is immense because the former directly misappropriates Scripture while the latter operates in concert with God. In the former sense, we lose sight of the objective, possibly bringing ruin on ourselves while the in the latter case, we *truly* operate like David who, when going against Goliath, so rightly deduced that he was coming against Goliath *in the name of the Lord*. But it wasn't just in the name of the Lord that David appropriated, it was also the *Will* of the Lord that was being worked out and that is why it was successful. This is in direct contrast to King Saul who gave lip service to God while looking at ways for self aggrandizement. This ultimately led to his downfall, his removal from the throne and ultimately his death. Sometimes the differences are so subtle that we fail to recognize that it is *us* driving the locomotive. Campus Crusade, in their four spiritual laws, recognized one thing that is very important and that is that Christians oftentimes remove God from the throne and place themselves on it, And while that is happening they fail to see that their lives are fruitless, that they could be more fulfilled if only they let God remain on the throne. Frankly, I always thought that these four spiritual laws were better suited for believers than unbelievers. It's the believers who misapply the principles of scripture and let themselves sit on the throne. If believers adopted the attitude, that God needs to be on the throne, then unbelievers could see the difference and they too could overcome the barriers to belief.

No Fear! On the one hand this attitude can lead to irrational destructive behavior; yet on the other hand, it can lead to a positive fulfilling life. If I were pressed on defining as to how one can know whether or not one is on the right track in trying to determine if it's him/her or God doing the directing here I would simply summarize it as follows: If you have to ask the question then it's likely not God, it's you! So if you're not sure then get back to the prayer closet until you are sure as to where the direction is coming from. The bottom line is this, even if you're not convinced that God is in control of the Universe and the details therein; if you spend enough time looking at your fears, at their roots and how they might be addressed then you have a good chance of overcoming them. This is certainly a better approach than just arbitrarily looking your fear in the eye and saying *I'm going after you and I'm going conquer you if it's the last thing I'm going to do.* You know, if you approach it with that attitude, without working through some of the basics it just might be the last thing you do. So, as a Christian you work through things, deliberately, contemplatively. And as God moves, you can address and even conquer those demons that seem to harbor in each and every one of us.

By the time I got to this part of the book I noticed one underlying theme that seems to permeate and weave its way through my thinking. *Most things in life require time. There is very little that can be accomplished without first thinking through the issues. And if you think an issue through, if you work through possible scenarios, consequences, then no matter what you do in life, you're* going to have a better chance of dealing with the results. As long you act first, then think later, life will always be a serious of highs and lows coupled with interminable frustration both as a human being and as a believer. No fear, works a lot better when God is on your side when you've only got a rock and a sling than if you've got a nuclear bomb and God is not with you!

CHAPTER TWENTY

THERE'S WORDS AND
THEN THERE'S WORDS

When talking to Christians, it is always a touchy subject to talk about balance in one's life. So many fundamentalist believers maintain that only fanatics are real Christians and that if you're not a fanatic then you might not be a *real* Christian. (Italics are mine). The difficulty with this notion is multifold and really becomes indicative of the decline of the critical thinking processes of present society.

The first problem lies in the use, at least mentally, of the word *fanatic*. Most individuals use this word in a negative sense. For example, news people will refer to fundamentalist, right wing believers as *fanatics*. The implication in this sense infers something akin to being of unsound mind, somewhat off balance, lights on, nobody home, etc. Interestingly enough this is really a misuse of the word itself, whose root comes from the word *fan*. As we all know, a *fan* is somebody who is strongly attracted to someone or something. In no way should this word be construed as a negative but it is, so we have to live with it. How, we misapply words and meanings associated with those words is a real problem in our society.

George Roche, in his book, *A World without Heroes*, spends a lot of time talking about our usage of the English language, how we indiscriminately use words and then how people perceive those words differently. It is to our advantage to be as precise as possible when we use words. After all, what you think I said may not be what I think you thought I did in fact say! To that extent the question of words plays a large role in our lives and indeed affects the issue of balance.

When I speak of balance, it is not to imply that we should sit on the fence. When I speak of balance I'm speaking of being sure of what is being communicated both in the delivery as well as the reception. To that end balance implies both a thoughtful process as well as a judicious choice within that process. Too often in our society we use the word Christian - sometimes it is used as a noun and other times it is used in adjective form.

Now what is a Christian? In some parts of the world a Christian is everybody. These countries have made Christianity a direct part of the culture and hence everybody born in that country is automatically a Christian. In Germany for example, you are either born Catholic or Lutheran. The only distinction is that - otherwise you are a Christian. In the United States there are several general meanings attached to that word. In a generic sense most people refer to themselves as Christians, even though they may not hold any specific religious values. So unless they hold specific views to the contrary these individuals call themselves Christians. Now if these people are asked about those who adhere to basic fundamental truths about Christianity then the word *fanatic* comes into play. Or words such as fundamentalist, evangelical, charismatic, are used as adjectives to describe the individual. The unfortunate part of this is that the word Christian has become dissected to such a point that it no longer holds any meaning. It's like Coke or Xerox. Because there are so many different soft drinks available and so many different types of copiers it is much more definitive, or general, just to talk about sodas or copies. At least you can't get into definition problems that way.

We have the same problem with the word Christian. Who are we talking about when we go down this trail? A Baptist? A Methodist? A Pentecostal? A Fundamentalist? An Evangelical? Who? To that extent I have concluded that the use of the word believer certainly comes closer to the truth of what I believe. Even thought I may be a spirit filled, evangelical, fundamentalist, conservative, Bible carrying Christian, I am really a Believer. That is probably the only way that I can say with certainty to the world of who I am.

Additionally, besides the noun Christian, we also have a tendency to use the word Christian in an adjectival form. For example, a Christian lawyer, a Christian doctor, a Christian school, Christian radio, Christian television, Christian books, whatever. There are some real difficulties with using the word Christian in this sense. The difficulty arises in that these words are used to conjure something in a person's mind, making it seem as if it is different when in reality there is no difference. Let me explain.

First, do you know what an *oxymoron* is? An *oxymoron* is the usage of two words which when put together, upon examination, are really contradictory. Without offending anybody, and with due respect I'll use the example of an *honest lawyer*. Now many lawyers have the reputation of being interested in only one thing, and that is to get something for their clients. Oftentimes it is at the expense of someone else. Now because these are usually win-lose situations, the loser generally blames the lawyer for the winning side for using unfair tactics, or whatever. Because of this reputation, lawyers have been labeled, over a period of time (sometimes justified, sometimes not) as being dishonest; After all the only real job for a lawyer is to win for his client. So when you say an individual is an *honest lawyer* you are doing one of two things; either you are saying that this is the only lawyer that is not scheming, conniving, lying, etc. or you are being facetious in that you really don't believe it and you are contradicting yourself in the use of these two words.

We use the word Christian in front of nouns, as adjectives, so commonly that it no longer has any meaning. Do you really care if the doctor is a Christian? Or, the plumber, or the A/C guy, or the pilot? Why do we care? If the pilot begins his flight by telling you he's a Christian, does that make him a better pilot? Or do you wonder if he's up in the cockpit reading his Bible while he should be watching the dials and gauges?

You see, we have made this whole issue of one word, *Christian*, such an insignificant word because we use it so much that it now has become meaningless. I finally got to the point that if somebody identifies himself as Christian early on in the process of establishing the relationship that I start looking for signs as to why he/she is telling me that. My wife constantly reminds me that words are just that, words. Let the word *Christian* drop from your vocabulary, and let the actions speak for themselves. If a repairman has to get his business by advertising in Christian Yellow Pages, I would begin questioning as to how good a repairman he is. Can't he survive, with his skills in the world at large? Is it only the *Christian* community that will let him survive? When was the last time a *Christian* repairman took you for a ride? Either he charged too much, or the job was lousy? How did you handle it? Poorly, I'm sure. If you complained you likely were made to feel guilty and then he badmouthed you to others. On the other hand, if you didn't complain you probably badmouthed this individual to others. In either case neither of you represented Jesus very well in your lives.

To the extent that I can, I have developed the personal philosophy that I deal with people who give me fair value for a job well done. If there's a problem, I deal with it. Everything is up-front, including what it's going to cost. Frankly, I'd rather not know if the guy is a Christian or Buddhist? Just do the job, the way I want it done. Don't be sucked into this philosophy that a Christian *whatever or whomever* is going to automatically treat you fairly. The responsibility to do your homework with regards to what you need in your professional dealings is yours, and yours alone. Using the adjectival form of *Christian* is merely an invitation to be subject to the whim and mercy of unscrupulous individuals whose only motive is money and we all know that there are plenty of those kind of individuals around. Does this mean you reject people who fall in this category? Of course not. Myself, when I consider getting a professional to do a job I look for the best person that I kind find and if this individual is a believer then that's a bonus.

Words, they are used so flippantly, so indiscriminately. We use them to convey messages and meanings and yet oftentimes don't consider the ramifications of their usage. James had a good handle on this notion of the tongue. It can be used for good but unbridled it can do so much damage. Unfortunately, we only view this in negative contexts such as deliberate usages to deceive or to hurt but it really goes much deeper than that. It is the context of language, when it confuses rather than enlightens, that the tongue create the most damage and we must keep that in mind. It is not always the obvious circumstances that create the difficulties, it is in those everyday situations, when we speak without thinking that we create the deepest rifts and hurts.

A final discourse on this subject is the very issue of words. Left unto themselves, words are just that - words. While they can be used for good or for bad, depending upon the source as well as the subject of the words there is another angle that is important to look at for a moment. Don't let your words, the ones that you really do choose to use, be idle. By themselves words are really only the initial foray into life. To be effective they must be associated with action. After you saunter down the highway of open mouth syndrome be sure that your actions correspond to the words that you have used. It's not enough that you judiciously select the appropriate word for the moment; it must be associated with action. For too long Christians have misapplied words in their everyday discourse and then still do nothing to confirm what is really behind them.

Jesus was a master at using words judiciously. And each word conveyed the meaning that he intended. Furthermore, his actions were demonstrable of the words that he had so carefully selected. For example, when he chased the money changers out of the Temple, his actions were directly associated with what he said. No more, no less. I think of James admonition in James 3:5 - *...the tongue is a small part of the body, but it makes great boasts. Consider what a great forest is set on fire by a small spark.* Now I know that most of this chapter deals with the unbridles use of the tongue and all the issues that go with that. Over the years, however, I have heard or read very little about much is associated with this usage of the tongue, namely action!. And that ultimately becomes the source of our greatest defeat as Believers; we are more concerned about saying the right thing, albeit through injudicious choice of words that we forget that we are called to action.

When we choose the words, the phrase, the sentence, it is then that we are called to let our being conform to that usage. If we speak love, we must do love or be love. If we speak standing up for our beliefs then we must be believers or do belief. If we speak right we must do right or be right. If we speak righteousness we must do righteousness or be righteousness. Otherwise, it is only words that we say and nobody knows who we are. I have often been accused of saying the right words in the right situation but then turning away and being the normal person that I have been perceived to be. Yes, perception is reality! And, no, people do not judge us by what we say but by who we are! Words are empty without the corresponding being, the corresponding action associated with them. I previously stated that it is important that your *aye be aye, and that your nay be nay.* That exhortation still stands. Without this consistency our words will always ring hollow. Jesus is often referred to as Love in its purest form. We generally do not argue about this as nobody can or would do for us what he did when he went on that cross. At the same time John 1:1 opens with these words... *In the beginning was the Word, and the Word was with God and the Word was God*. The concept of Words and Love, all summed up in Jesus! Interesting notion, isn't it? The very idea that our very being is tied up in love and words, those ideas that can create or destroy. And we spend so little time in choosing our Words along with the corresponding action. In 1 Corinthians 13: 1 we read that *if I speak in the tongues of men and of angels, but have not love, I am only a resounding gong or a clanging cymbal*. Words and Love, bound up in me, in you. And yet we still don't understand the emptiness that we ourselves create when we don't take the time to choose our words correctly and then be what we say. It is no wonder that the emptiness in our lives, caused by meaningless words uttered over the course of our lives, threatens to make us deaf by its roar! And it threatens to erase the only potential meaning that we could possibly apprehend.

CHAPTER TWENTY ONE

THE SUM OF ALL FEARS

One thing that I have learned over the course of my life is that it is impossible to come on the correct answer unless I first learn to ask the right questions. As so often happens we leap at the first opportunity to jump into the fight, whatever the fight may happen to be. Usually without benefit of first thinking through the issues and the possible solutions. I sincerely hope that the previous chapters at least spur your thought processes to ask the right questions if you are frustrated in your present spiritual journey. There is no question in my mind that any of the issues discussed couldn't be addressed in one book by themselves. But then the purpose of this exercise was really to spur you onward to ask the questions, to see if you have the right internal stuff to move through the confusing maze of everything that is being offered to you as a believer. And the right stuff in this situation is not meant to imply anything other than your own desire to really move forward in faith. Our lives, afterall, are difficult enough without having our faith becoming a stumbling block in our efforts to get to the truth which will ultimately set us free.

The previous chapter entitled There's words and then there's words is really an excellent lead-in for this final chapter. After all is said and done there needs to be some closure if we are to resolve the sum of our fears and move forward in our lives as believers. And the closure begins here. Throughout the course of this book I have attempted to hit on those issues that

I have sensed as being critical to the spiritual dimension of the 20th Century believer as we prepare to move into the next millennium. That sounds so ominous, doesn't it? Moving into the next millennium. Especially in light of the staggering changes that affect us daily. Throughout the course of this book I have attempted to write from the heart, not as an academic or as if I were empowered with a new message. After all, one can't improve on the perfect message that we have been given though Jesus Christ. There is no question that our faith is in crisis, that we believers are being hammered from all directions. And under this deluge of conflicting pressures we are not only pressed to engage our God in a positive, uplifting relationship but we are, at the same time, facing unbelievable pressures to live and work, indeed survive and prosper in a world that by many measures seems to be spinning out of control.

This state of affairs is, however, nothing new to Christianity. We have always been forced to re-evaluate our faith in light of societal development. The social, economic and spiritual issues that believers have faced over the past millennia have always ultimately led to a more dynamic relationship with the living God, to the one whose name we claim. So whether we look retrospectively to the dark ages, the middle ages, the Reformation period or the many rapid changes that we have experienced over the past 100 years, the changes have generally been positive and affirming.

Yet as I gaze onto the current religious landscape I do find myself fearful for the future. I sense that our new rapid, technologically developing world has created a general climate whereby this generation may become identified as that generation which is responsible for the extinction of Christianity as we know it. Think about it. We've put men on the moon and are contemplating the secrets of the Universe. At the same time the development of the cyberspace concept threatens to make personal relationships obsolete. The very social fabric of our society is threatened as the man-machine (computer) relationship becomes more important than the man-man relationship. And as more people begin to telecommute to the workplace as opposed to going to work, the personal relationships among people will erode even further. And this in a world where personal relationships are already at all time low. Yet, somehow, in this milieu we must still deal with God the ultimate creator the Universe, and the author and finisher of our Faith.

In many ways I perceive our present condition akin to what is recorded in Genesis as men built the Tower of Babel in an attempt to physically reach God, the sense being that if man could reach him who didn't reach down then God could be co-opted. I sense that our present world is trying to do the very same thing - reach to the very stars to apprehend God, yet not realizing that it is God who does the apprehending. And under this blanket of frenetic behavior we see humanity struggling with deep rooted spiritual issues, eliciting the sense that we must have this spiritual cognition in our hand, when we encounter this God, this all powerful one when we finally do reach him. And so in our frantic rushing around we look for quicker solutions and the perfect formula to immediately access this creator of the Universe. Yet under this veneer of we can do it lurks the despair of no access to the one to who we place our allegiance. Yes, there is a crisis. Our present belief system, as refined and passed down by our spiritual forefathers has been threatened by man's all consuming desire to achieve. No longer do we want to study the scriptures with wisdom in mind. Nor do we want to pray with the intent of building relationships, only to get.

And out of this intense desire for NOW we ultimately conclude, either consciously or subconsciously, that our faith is not only not durable but also unreasonable in the light of the new world that we are so diligently creating. The relationship with the one who redeemed certainly seems to fade. And when we do trod down the road of faith the notion of instant reward always seems to be the primary condition for the measurement of truth. If that does not meet our expectations then we move on. In our society 50% of marriages currently fail, they end in divorce and many move on to engage in a sort of serial monogamy. And so it is with our Faith. We move from one church to another, from one God to another, really practicing a serial monotheism as the God in each church seems to be just a little different from the one left behind. Is it any wonder then, then the words *durable* and *reasonable* play a very limited role in our walk of faith?

What about these two words - *durable* and *reasonable*. Let's examine them in light of our changing world. There is no question in my mind that our faith is still as durable as ever. Two thousand years of history certainly validate the durability of our faith even if we have more questions than answers. And I believe that we have spoken to many of the questions that you may have, to the issues that confront us as believers. God has not forsaken his creation; even in the light of our current frantic behavior he has never left our presence. If you need a reminder, read Hebrews 11 and the great roll call of Faith. And then reflect on those whose blood was shed over the centuries so that we might enjoy what we so take for granted. Do not fret and dwell over the anxiety that our present circumstances press on us. He still does move stones!

At the same time our faith is still reasonable. In addition to moving stones, he still restores sight to the blind, hearing to the deaf, the ability to walk to the lame. He heals the sick, restores the soul, and gives to those who ask - a new heart. Even after these thousands of years, he has not changed! No matter how hard we try to force new rules on the game it does not change his basic instructions; they are still as clear as the day he changed forever his relationship to his creation. The reasonableness of God's victory through Christ is firmly entrenched in his creation in the here and now. We must constantly remember that that He came to us - we didn't go to him! So the expectation must be that it is in the 'here' that we will continue to meet him as we journey into and through the next millennium. We cannot expedite his coming again, nor can we force another incarnation of sorts. We simply do not have that mandate from him, no matter how good we think we are. Nonetheless, it is clear, that in the 3000 years since God first spoke to Abraham, his message that we must walk by faith, not sight is not only a durable exhortation but a reasonable expectation.

Not only does the durability and reasonableness of our faith need to be examined in light of our expectations but these concepts must be viewed as tools. In and of themselves, tools are merely inanimate objects that convey no power. In and of themselves, they do not produce or create anything. In the hands of a craftsman, however, a hammer and saw can be used to build something. A brush can used by an artist to create a Mona Lisa that transcends the centuries. A story can be used by a master story teller to pass on the heritage of one generation to the next. And as God's creation, as believers, Faith is our tool whereby we transcend this three dimensional world of worries and hurts and frustrations and anxiety.

Yes, our faith is a tool. It is durable and reasonable. More importantly, it is available if we but ask. It does not exist in a vacuum but is an instrument that must be picked up and used each and every moment of every day. Faith does not come equipped with an instruction manual that bypasses skills honed over a period of time and use. On the one hand it is the easiest of all known tools to be picked up yet it is the last one that we learn to use properly. It is the most powerful gift that God gives us but the most underutilized tool in our repertoire. So easy, yet so hard. So apprehensible but so incomprehensible! And in our world of the NOW, this Faith, this tool for our very survival is the only assurance we have that we can will overcome. Arise, shine, for the light has come! The glory of the Lord has risen! Even in the darkness of these times, even in the anxiety of a world gone mad, our faith in him is still durable, reasonable and practicable. He still moves stones and transplants hearts. Even in our fears he is present.